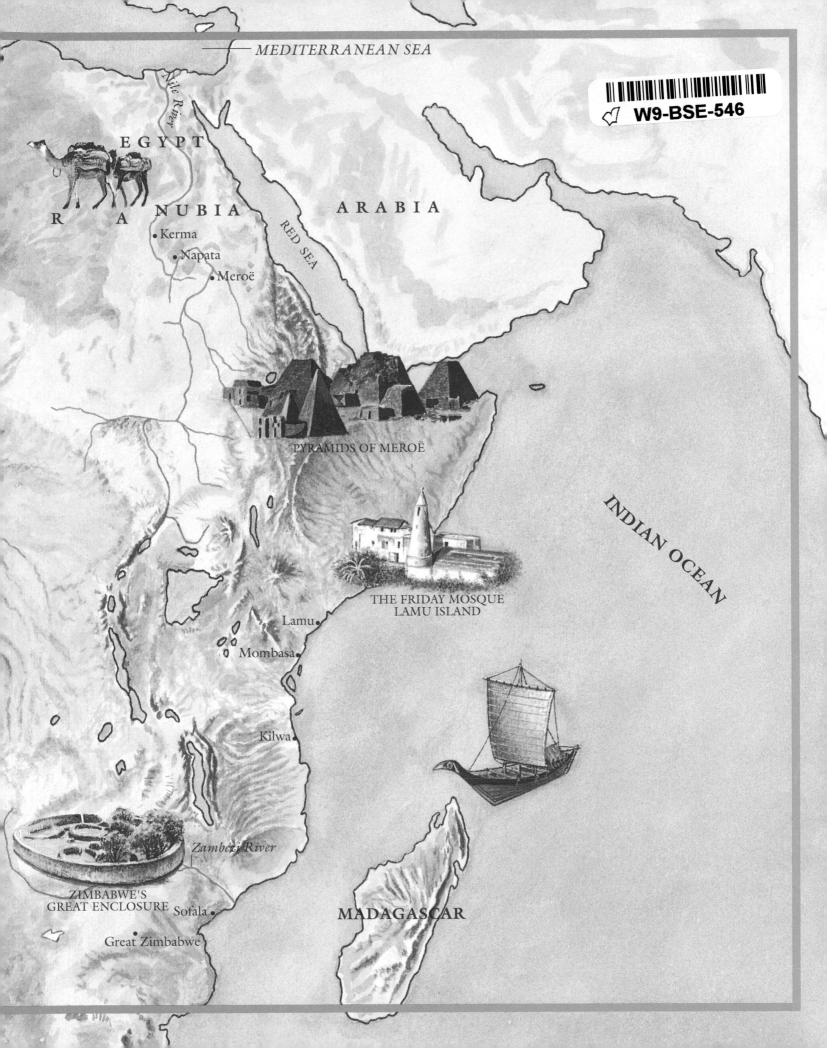

MEDITERRANEAN SEA

Nile River

EGYPT

NUBIA

ARABIA

RED SEA

• Kerma

• Napata

• Meroë

PYRAMIDS OF MEROË

INDIAN OCEAN

THE FRIDAY MOSQUE
LAMU ISLAND

Lamu •

Mombasa •

Kilwa •

Zambezi River

ZIMBABWE'S
GREAT ENCLOSURE   Sofala •

Great Zimbabwe

MADAGASCAR

Cover: A cast-brass head from the West African kingdom of Benin is displayed against a backdrop of the steeply angled stone pyramids of Jebel Barkal, a religious center of ancient Kush, in modern-day Sudan. The head was worn as a hip ornament by Benin chiefs and other high-ranking persons to fasten the elaborate skirts worn during palace ceremonies.

End paper: Painted by the artist Paul Breeden, the map shows the continent of Africa and some of the artifacts and monuments that make up its glorious legacy. Breeden also painted the vignettes illustrating the timeline on pages 158-159.

AFRICA'S GLORIOUS LEGACY

Time-Life Books is a division of TIME LIFE INC.

PRESIDENT and CEO: John M. Fahey, Jr.

EDITOR-IN-CHIEF: John L. Papanek

TIME-LIFE BOOKS

MANAGING EDITOR: Roberta Conlan

Executive Art Director: Ellen Robling
Director of Photography and Research:
John Conrad Weiser
Senior Editors: Russell B. Adams, Jr., Dale M.
Brown, Janet Cave, Lee Hassig, Robert
Somerville, Henry Woodhead
Director of Technology: Eileen Bradley
Director of Editorial Operations:
Prudence G. Harris

PRESIDENT: John D. Hall

Vice President, Director of Marketing:
Nancy K. Jones
Vice President, New Product Development:
Neil Kagan
Production Manager: Marlene Zack
Supervisor of Quality Control: James King

Editorial Operations
Production: Celia Beattie
Library: Louise D. Forstall
Computer Composition: Deborah G. Tait
(Manager), Monika D. Thayer, Janet Barnes
Syring, Lillian Daniels

**Library of Congress
Cataloging in Publication Data**
Africa's glorious legacy / by the editors of
Time-Life Books.
    p. cm.—(Lost civilizations)
Includes bibliographical references and index.
ISBN 0-8094- 9025-0 (trade)
ISBN 0-8094- 9026-9 (library)
1. Excavations (Archaeology)—Africa.
2. Africa—Antiquities.
3. Africa—Civilization.
I. Time-Life Books. II. Series.
DT13.A37 1994   94-916
960'.1—dc20

LOST CIVILIZATIONS

SERIES EDITOR: Dale Brown
Administrative Editor: Philip Brandt George

Editorial staff for *Africa's Glorious Legacy*
Art Director: Susan K. White
Picture Editor: Charlotte Fullerton
Text Editors: James Lynch (principal),
Russell B. Adams, Jr., Charlotte Anker,
Denise Dersin, Charles J. Hagner
Associate Editors/Research-Writing: Robin
Currie, Katherine L. Griffin, Dan Kulpinski,
Patricia Mitchell
Senior Copyeditor: Jarelle S. Stein
Picture Coordinator: David Herod
Editorial Assistant: Patricia D. Whiteford

Special Contributors: Ellen Galford, Donál K.
Gordon, Norman Kolpas, Barbara Mallen
(text); Maureen L. Deuser, Ann-Louise G.
Gates, Gail Prensky, Bonnie Stutski, Elizabeth
Thompson (research/writing); Roy Nanovic
(index)

Correspondents: Elisabeth Kraemer-Singh
(Bonn), Christine Hinze (London), Christina
Lieberman (New York), Maria Vincenza Aloisi
(Paris), Ann Natanson (Rome).
Valuable assistance was also provided by Nihal
Tamraz (Cairo), Ian Mills (Harare), Peter
Hawthorne (Johannesburg), Judy Aspinall
(London), Saskia van de Linde (Netherlands),
Ann Wise (Rome), Bogdan Turek (Warsaw).

The Consultants:
Timothy Kendall is associate curator, department of Egyptian and Ancient Near Eastern Art at the Museum of Fine Arts in Boston. He is author of numerous articles on the archaeology of Africa and was director of the Museum of Fine Arts Archaeological Mission at Jebel Barkal in the Sudan.

David Killick earned two B.A.s from the University of Cape Town and a masters degree and Ph.D. in anthropology from Yale University. Now teaching at the University of Arizona, he is an expert in the later prehistory and early history of Africa with a special interest in technological innovation.

Adria LaViolette teaches in the Carter G. Woodson Institute for Afro-American and African Studies at the University of Virginia. She has extensive archaeological field experience in Mali and Tanzania.

Roderick James McIntosh, professor of anthropology at Rice University, is a West African specialist. He has more than 20 years field experience at numerous sites, including Begho, Ghana; Djoulde Djabe, Senegal; and Timbuktu, Dia, and Jenné-jeno in Mali.

Emily Teeter is assistant curator at the Oriental Institute Museum at the University of Chicago. Long associated with studies and exhibits concerning Egypt and Nubia, she curated the Oriental Institute's exhibit *Vanished Kingdoms of the Nile: The Rediscovery of Ancient Nubia.*

Other Publications:
WEIGHT WATCHERS® SMART
  CHOICE RECIPE COLLECTION
TRUE CRIME
THE AMERICAN INDIANS
THE ART OF WOODWORKING
ECHOES OF GLORY
THE NEW FACE OF WAR
HOW THINGS WORK
WINGS OF WAR
CREATIVE EVERYDAY COOKING
COLLECTOR'S LIBRARY OF
  THE UNKNOWN
CLASSICS OF WORLD WAR II
TIME-LIFE LIBRARY OF CURIOUS
  AND UNUSUAL FACTS
AMERICAN COUNTRY
VOYAGE THROUGH THE UNIVERSE
THE THIRD REICH
THE TIME-LIFE GARDENER'S GUIDE
MYSTERIES OF THE UNKNOWN
TIME FRAME
FIX IT YOURSELF
FITNESS, HEALTH & NUTRITION
SUCCESSFUL PARENTING
HEALTHY HOME COOKING
UNDERSTANDING COMPUTERS
LIBRARY OF NATIONS
THE ENCHANTED WORLD
THE KODAK LIBRARY OF
  CREATIVE PHOTOGRAPHY
GREAT MEALS IN MINUTES
THE CIVIL WAR
PLANET EARTH
COLLECTOR'S LIBRARY OF
  THE CIVIL WAR
THE EPIC OF FLIGHT
THE GOOD COOK
WORLD WAR II
HOME REPAIR AND IMPROVEMENT
THE OLD WEST

*For information on and a full description of
any of the Time-Life Books series listed above,
please call 1-800-621-7026 or write:*
Reader Information
Time-Life Customer Service
P.O. Box C-32068
Richmond, Virginia 23261-2068

This volume is one in a series that explores the worlds of the past, using the finds of archaeologists and other scientists to bring ancient peoples and their cultures vividly to life.

Other volumes in the series include:

AFRICA'S GLORIOUS LEGACY

By the Editors of Time-Life Books

TIME-LIFE BOOKS, ALEXANDRIA, VIRGINIA

C O N T E N T S

OPENING THE DOOR ON AFRICA'S PAST

With only a vague idea of what lay ahead of him, Karl Mauch set out on foot across South Africa's great Central Plateau on May 9, 1871. The young German geologist had planned this trek the year before, while he was recuperating from a bout of malaria in a missionary outpost. There Mauch had met a fellow German, the Reverend A. Merensky, who had stirred his imagination with tales of a colossal stone ruin that lay somewhere in the gold fields to the north. Now, with a double-barreled shotgun over his shoulder and an oversize parasol tilted against the blazing South African sun, Mauch headed off into Mashonaland—the ancestral home of the Shona people.

Actually, though Mauch did not know it, there were hundreds of stone ruins in the region. The Shona called them *dzimba woye,* literally "venerated houses" in their language. (The name, transliterated into English as *zimbabwe,* was adopted in 1980 by the independent African nation that encompasses most of these remarkable sites.) The ruins had come to the attention of the Portuguese —the first Europeans to circumnavigate Africa—more than 300 years before and had been misidentified, misinterpreted, and mistreated many times since then.

Sixteenth-century Portuguese explorers and missionaries heard and repeated rumors linking the ruins they called Symbaoe to

Covered with ornamental tattoos or scarification lines, this 4½-inch clay figure of a wide-hipped female was fashioned some 4,000 years ago by one of Nubia's earliest civilizations, the so-called C-group.

the biblical tales of King Solomon and the queen of Sheba. Some felt Mashonaland was the legendary Ophir, described in the Old Testament. King Solomon, so the story goes, built a fleet of ships "which brought gold from Ophir, and precious stones." Down the years, these stories circulated—and gained credence—throughout Europe and would be clung to with special fervor by fundamentalist Dutch immigrants who began settling in South Africa in the 17th century.

Inspired by such romantic visions—and by dreams of wealth—Mauch tramped through the bush for four months in search of the ruins. In late August he found shelter in the home of Adam Render, a German trader who lived with two African wives in the heart of the gold country. While there, Mauch was told of "quite large ruins," two and a half hours distant, which, according to Mauch's journal entry, "could never have been built by Blacks."

Four days later, accompanied by Shona guides, Mauch at last came upon a solitary hill with bare granite outcrops poking through the green vegetation. "Presently I stood before it and beheld a wall of a height of about 20 feet of granite bricks. Very close by there was a place where a kind of foot-path led over rubble into the interior. Following this path I stumbled over masses of rubble and parts of walls and dense thickets. I stopped in front of a towerlike structure. Altogether it rose to a height of about 30 feet." He was amazed to find that these colossal walls had been built without mortar.

With far more emotional fervor than scholarly reserve, Karl Mauch immediately began speculating on the ruin's history. He uncovered a soapstone bowl and an iron gong, which he took as proof that "a civilized nation must once have lived here." Most telling, however, was the sliver of wood that Mauch trimmed from a crossbeam over the northern entrance to the grandest ruin, known to the Shona as "the House of the Great Wife" (called the Hill Ruin today).

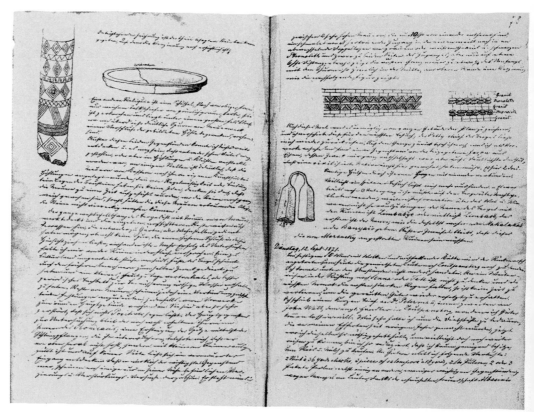

Mistakenly thinking that he had found the biblical queen of Sheba's capital city of Ophir, German geologist and explorer Karl Mauch mapped the crumbling granite walls of Great Zimbabwe in 1871. Like many scholars who followed him, Mauch was too prejudiced to believe that the imposing structures could have been built by Africans.

These pages from Karl Mauch's journal of September 11, 1871, depict the three artifacts—and some decorative stone friezes—that he discovered at Great Zimbabwe. From left to right, they include a section of a soapstone monolith, a cracked soapstone dish, and a double iron gong.

The wood—fragrant, reddish, and like the wood of a pencil—seemed to be cedar, which, Mauch deduced, "cannot come from anywhere else but from the Libanon." Furthermore, he averred, "only the Phoenicians could have brought it here; Salomo [Solomon] used a lot of cedar wood for the building of his palaces. Including here the visit of the Queen of Seba [Sheba], one gets as a result that the great woman who built the *rondeau* could have been none other than the Queen of Seba."

Mauch's fanciful summation found a rapt audience among South Africa's white colonists. The British South Africa Company, headed by the wealthy Cecil Rhodes, sought to lend the weight of scientific authority to Mauch's theory. Rhodes invited the antiquities expert James Theodore Bent to examine the site, which came to be known as Great Zimbabwe. Bent firmly believed that the builders of Great Zimbabwe hailed from somewhere outside of Africa, and he was initially dismayed at the lack of resemblance between these ruins and any architectural style associated with the Bible. When cursory digging in the stone enclosures turned up only a few crude potsherds, copper spearheads, and gold-working crucibles—all clearly of African origin—Bent was moved to confess, "I have not much faith in the antiquity of these ruins; I think they are native."

But soon Bent changed his mind again. Four soapstone birds found atop carved monoliths inside one fortresslike structure suggested to him connections with Assyria, Mycenae, Cyprus, Egypt, and Phoenicia. He quickly began to see other ancient parallels in the ruins' towering walls, leading him to his final, satisfying judgment that "a northern race closely akin to the Phoenician and Egyptian" had built Great Zimbabwe. To Bent, it seems, almost anyone in the ancient world could have erected these magnificent structures—anyone, that is, except the Africans who lived around them.

Soon after Mauch's and Bent's forays, a slew of treasure hunters descended upon the ruins. In their quest for ancient exotica, the looters destroyed most of the valuable indicators archaeologists might have used for a scientific study of the site. Some of the most damaging work was done by Richard Hall, who was given the title curator of Great Zimbabwe by Cecil Rhodes's British South Africa Company in 1902. (By then Mashonaland had been annexed outright by the British and renamed Rhodesia in honor of the famous industrialist.) In his efforts to rid the site of the "filth and decadence" of the later Shona inhabitants, Hall removed up to 12 feet of

stratified deposits from the enclosures. This proved to be too much, even for those licentious times; his tenure lasted a brief two years.

In 1905 the British Association for the Advancement of Science, hoping for irrefutable evidence of Great Zimbabwe's non-African heritage, commissioned the well-respected archaeologist David Randall-MacIver to conduct a full and systematic excavation of the ruins. Though hard-pressed to find undisturbed deposits for his study, Randall-MacIver was able to determine that the domestic pottery from all the strata—from the earliest, coinciding with the construction of the stone walls, to the most recent—was closely related to the pottery of the contemporary Shona. There were also some obvious foreign imports at the site—Chinese porcelain and Arabian glass—but the overwhelming majority of artifacts clearly appeared to be indigenous.

Thus Randall-MacIver concluded that Great Zimbabwe was "unquestionably African in every detail," adding soberly that "many will bewail that a romance has been destroyed. But surely it is a prosaic mind that sees no romance in the partial opening of this new chapter in the history of vanished cultures. A corner is lifted of

Richard Hall, a British journalist named curator of Great Zimbabwe in 1902, inspects the crumbling walls with a cane-wielding colleague, Franklin Wright. Hall's study of the site led him mistakenly to proclaim that Arab traders had constructed the massive stone buildings.

that veil which has shrouded the forgotten but not unrecoverable past of the African negro."

Randall-MacIver's pronouncement ignited a firestorm of controversy that raged for more than a generation. In 1929, still unable to forge a consensus of opinion about Great Zimbabwe's builders, the British Association recruited another eminent archaeologist, Gertrude Caton-Thompson, to reexamine the ruins. Caton-Thompson's investigations—exhaustive, meticulous, and scientifically exemplary in every detail—led her to state unequivocally, "The ruins are, in my opinion, indigenous in a full sense of the term."

Neither David Randall-MacIver's nor Gertrude Caton-Thompson's judgments quelled the debate: Bent, Hall, and the majority Western opinion of that period simply would not concede that Africans were capable of greatness. To be sure, ancient Egypt's achievements were revered, and, technically, Egypt was a part of Africa. Still, that seemed more like geographical chance. Egypt, with its access to the Mediterranean, was thought of as part of that world, and the dazzling glory of the pharaohs blinded people to what lay beyond. In the thinking of those times, civilization ended at Aswan, and the rest of Africa was a land without a past.

This attitude among whites had been centuries in the making. In his *Philosophy of History,* published in 1854, the influential German sophist Georg Wilhelm Hegel had offered the view that "Africa is not an historical continent; it shows neither change nor development, and whatever may have happened there belongs to the world of Asia and of Europe." Likewise, a century earlier, Scottish philosopher David Hume unhesitatingly pronounced that black Africans have "no ingenious manufactures among them, no arts, no sciences." Such deeply ingrained prejudice dies hard: As late as 1961 Hugh Trevor Roper, distinguished regius professor of history at Oxford, said, "At present there is no African history: there is only the history of the Europeans in Africa. The rest is darkness."

And yet, if one goes back far enough, a striking contrast to the misguided presumptions of Hegel, Hume, and Roper can be seen in white attitudes toward black Africa. Indeed, to the Greeks and Romans, the lands south of the Sahara were places of magic and wonder, peopled with great warriors and beautiful queens.

Some later accounts are equally laudatory. In the 14th century AD, the Muslim theologian and world traveler

British archaeologist Gertrude Caton-Thompson conducted systematic excavations at Great Zimbabwe in 1929. Her findings, published two years later, overturned the common notion that the structures must have been erected by non-African colonists.

11

Ibn Battuta visited Mali, a vast empire on the West African grasslands. Though the scholar had crossed two continents and visited more than 40 countries in 29 years of wandering, he was deeply impressed by what he saw: The emperor, enthroned under a domed pavilion of silk surmounted by a large bird of gold, presided over a realm unsurpassed in its civility. "Of all peoples, the Negroes are those who most abhor injustice," wrote Ibn Battuta. "The Sultan pardons no one who is guilty of it. There is complete and general safety throughout the land. The traveler here has no more reason than the man who stays at home to fear brigands, thieves or ravishers."

European societies of Ibn Battuta's time had little contact with sub-Saharan Africa. North African Muslims maintained an economic blockade to ensure their continued monopoly of the trans-Saharan trade. Nor could European mariners circumvent the desert barrier in their primitive sailing ships, since they lacked the ability to tack against the prevailing northerly winds along Africa's Atlantic coast. By the 15th century, however, improved navigational instruments and lateen sails enabled European seafarers to safely travel down the West African "bulge" into the Gulf of Guinea and beyond.

Scores of Europeans began putting ashore, lured by tales of fabulous wealth in the continent's interior. One such adventurer was Anselm d'Isalguier, who returned to Marseilles from West Africa in 1413 with a black princess for a wife and a retinue of servants. One of his African retainers, skilled in the medical arts, was called upon to treat the ailing Dauphin Charles, crown prince of France. Over the next two centuries, as Africa came to be better known, European views seemed, on the whole, to be untainted by racial bias. Dutch traders returning from the West African kingdom of Benin in the 17th century reported that the inhabitants were "people who have good laws and a well organized police; who live on good terms with the Dutch and other foreigners who come to trade among them, and to whom they show a thousand marks of friendship."

By the 18th century, however, such objectivity had given way to a none-too-subtle form of disinformation. Blacks were now portrayed as primitives devoid of the finer instincts and talents that foster humankind's nobler achievements. Racist sentiments such as these began to develop during Europe's industrial revolution. The technological dichotomy that arose in the 1700s between the two continents prompted a cultural bigotry as well. Africans were seen not just as primitive but as something less than human, a view that

ZIMBABWE

Despite Caton-Thompson's proof of Great Zimbabwe's African origins, a 1938 Rhodesian travel poster perpetuates the association of the ruin with the queen of Sheba. Here, her ghostly figure appears among the ruins and receives homage from a kneeling African, who is bearing a huge gold nugget.

played into—and seemed to morally justify—the vast and monstrous trans-Atlantic slave trade that eventually became a key enterprise in the commerce of the Western world.

Slavery in one form or another is ubiquitous throughout human history, and to be sure, the institution had long been accepted within traditional African societies. Slaves labored in the salt and copper mines and served as a vital link in the trans-Saharan trade routes, acting as porters in the forest regions where camels and donkeys could not go. They were tangible symbols of wealth for some of Africa's nobility. Additionally, slaves had for countless centuries constituted one of Africa's principle exports to the Greek, Roman, and eventually Arab worlds.

The idea of slavery, therefore, was not a new one to Africa; but the European concept of basing the entire agricultural economy of much of the New World on African slave labor proved to be devastating. Three centuries of ruthless traffic in millions of African men, women, and children unleashed an era of violence and instability in the interior of the continent. Many societies there fell into a long period of decline.

Lamentably, later Europeans never imagined that African culture had ever been any different. Said Georg Wilhelm Hegel, "Nothing remotely human is to be found in the Negro character. Their condition is capable of neither development nor education. As we see them today, so they have always been." The black man, added the 19th-century British author Anthony Trollope, makes "no approach to the civilization of his white fellow creatures, whom he imitates as a monkey does a man."

It would take Europeans a long time to revert to their much earlier—and much more accurate—assessment of Africa and its peoples. Thanks in no small measure to the work of open-minded archaeologists over the course of the last century, Africa is now universally recognized as the home of many fascinating indigenous cultures that have made numerous contributions to humankind's record of innovation and achievement.

Fossil evidence clearly indicates that Africa is the birthplace of the human species. From skull and bone fragments found at Olduvai Gorge and other sites in East Africa, anthropologists have determined that, about 1.5 million years ago, *Homo erectus* first strode across the region's open grasslands.

From this African genesis so long ago, humans fanned out to populate the entire planet over generations beyond number. Some scientists, citing genetic analysis of human DNA taken from a wide selection of races and ethnic groups, suggest that the earth's population can trace its origins back to a single African female. Though the conclusions of this study remain controversial, noted archaeologist Thurstan Shaw asserted in 1989, "Eve was an African."

Little is known of the eons between this "Eve" and the emergence of the world's earliest cultures. Sometime before the fifth millennium BC, however, the faint light of prehistory illuminates what were among Africa's first sophisticated Stone Age cultures. The evidence is mostly pictorial: In 1958 French explorer Henri Lhote discovered a series of superb rock paintings and engravings in the Sahara depicting hunters stalking large herds of long-horn cattle and lush valleys teeming with the exotic wildlife for which Africa is renown. Together with climatic evidence from geological deposits, the artworks point to a period in Africa's remote past when the Sahara was a well-watered garden with abundant wildlife, where hunter-gatherers, and later farmers and herders, created singular societies.

A gradual change in climate, however, had a devastating effect on the region's environment and on its inhabitants. The ancient lakes and rivers started to dry up. As the once verdant grasslands gave way to scrub and afterward to desert, the wild game in the area disappeared, and the human population dispersed into other, more accommodating climes.

Some went south to join the peoples already living in those tropical latitudes. These inhabitants of sub-Saharan Africa were now isolated by ocean on three sides and the world's largest desert on the fourth, just at the point in human history when the burgeoning civilizations of the ancient world were beginning to profit from expanded interaction among themselves, trading ideas and technology. Long distance transoceanic and trans-Saharan trade routes had not yet evolved, leaving but one natural thoroughfare to the outside world, the Nile River.

The northward flowing river pierced the desert barrier along

Dating from the prehistoric time when the Sahara was a lush region of rivers and grasslands, these rock paintings were discovered in one of the desert's central plateaus. Above, hunters armed with bows and arrows leap in pursuit of game; at right, herdsmen tend cattle, while women and children gather near huts and perform their own chores.

Africa's eastern flank, providing some give and take—via Egypt—between the civilizations of the Middle East and the cultures of Nubia on the Upper Nile, some 400 miles south of Memphis. In this way, for example, the Nubians probably learned to smelt iron.

This kind of technology transfer certainly benefited the Nubians, but it was a mere trickle compared to the flood of foreign techniques and products available to cosmopolitan Egypt through its Mediterranean and Middle Eastern connections. As an artery of crosscultural exchange for Africa as a whole, the Nile was more of a cul-de-sac than a conduit. More than those anywhere else in the the Old World, the peoples of sub-Saharan Africa would evolve in a vacuum, with only each other to learn from and depend on.

Sequestered though they were, the inhabitants of this immense and varied region developed cultures of great originality and diversity. And they did so in the face of climatic extremes: dank rain

forests, sunbaked savanna grasslands, searing desert, low-lying mangrove swamps, and glacier-capped mountains. Roughly 80 percent of the African landmass—everything between the Sahara and Kalahari Deserts—lies within the tropics, a far higher percentage than any other continent. There is awesome beauty to be found here, but the land also holds countless hazards that are endemic to the tropics—disease, blights, harmful bacteria and parasites, and an impressive array of hungry carnivores, biting insects, and poisonous snakes.

Despite such obstacles, the pioneer agriculturalists of Africa learned—on their own—to domesticate eight cereal and four root crops, supplementing them with nearly 40 additional species of cultivated plants. These skilled farmers also raised cattle, goats, and sheep and tracked wild game across the boundless hills, felling them with the bow and arrow—very probably an African invention. By the middle of the first millennium BC, people had learned to extract metals from the earth and refine them. With their newfound knowledge they crafted durable spears and tools.

Thus equipped, the inhabitants of sub-Saharan Africa became better farmers and hunters and eventually established settled communities. Between these villages, trade evolved, based on the barter of iron, salt, copper, and foodstuffs. In some areas with more productive agriculture or command of desirable resources, a portion of the populace could turn away from food production toward other pursuits. This division of labor—a prerequisite to the emergence of urban society—gave rise to a specialist class of merchants, artisans, and metalworkers. As the more warlike and ambitious of the groups exerted control over their weaker neighbors, city-states and kingdoms were born.

These political entities were as various in form and expression as the regions over which they held sway. In the grasslands of West Africa, the first of a string of mercantile towns appeared early in the first millennium AD, establishing early trade networks with the surrounding communities. They would eventually become part of the vast empire that grew rich on the exchange of gold and other precious commodities between the southern forest and the northern savanna.

Far to the east, along the Indian Ocean coast, powerful seaport cities built of coral developed around an ancient maritime trading culture—the Swahili—which from about the eighth century AD was importing pottery from the Persian Gulf, some of it for sale to the African interior. By the 10th century, in the arid grazing lands of the Zimbabwe Plateau, a number of independent, competing city-states—forebears of Great Zimbabwe—grew up based on the acquisition of cattle. Eventually, a vigorous and lucrative trading network would link them to the Swahili coast.

Onto this grand stage of political and cultural development appeared a new and sweeping force that would have dramatic and lasting ramifications for much of the African continent. The prophet Muhammad came to the fore in Arabia during the seventh century AD, and in the years following his death, the new faith he promulgated—Islam—spread rapidly throughout his homeland and far beyond. The peoples of North Africa were among the earliest converts. Consequently, as sub-Saharan African trade patterns expanded beyond regional boundaries—via an embryonic long-distance network across the Sahara and the Indian Ocean—West and East Africans came directly into contact with Islam.

Over time—and of their own volition—many African traders, both East and West, converted to the faith of their Arab associates. Since these traders constituted the rich and powerful elite of their societies, others followed their lead, and most African cities had a sizable Muslim population by the 13th century AD. Much later, in the 18th and 19th centuries, West African Muslims would embark on a jihad, or holy war, sweeping down across the savanna on their horses and converting West Africans en masse at sword point. Even now, the demarcation of Islam's purview in this region is roughly the line between grassland and forest, beyond which—owing to the prevalence of the tsetse fly—the Islamic horsemen could not penetrate.

But while many Africans adopted the Muslim faith, and even took on Arabic names, they remained thoroughly African in their outlook. The arrival of Islam did not obliterate the preexisting cultures, nor did it erase the autonomous African identity. Many of the African societies embraced Islam with fervor, then set about interpreting Muslim doctrine and practices to fit their own uniquely African circumstances. Sometimes the results were unrecognizable—and shocking—to an orthodox Muslim.

When Ibn Battuta arrived in Mali in the 14th century, he discovered that its peoples had been practicing Islam for more than 300 years. But the distinguished cleric was appalled to find that Mali's women—the sultan's daughters included—not only shunned the veil but went about totally naked. The gravity of the transgression—in this Arab observer's eyes—was offset somewhat by the piousness of the population. "On Fridays," he noted, "anyone who is late at the mosque will find nowhere to pray, the crowd is so great. They zealously learn the Koran by heart. Those children who are neglectful in this are put in chains until they have memorized the Koran."

Some of Africa's paramount achievements have occurred in the states, kingdoms, and empires where Islam has held sway. But the record of splendor in Africa predates that religion by more than two millennia, reaching back before the dawn of recorded history itself to that stretch of the Nile Valley that lies just south of Egypt.

Of Nubia, the home of many ancient civilizations, the Greek poet Homer wrote: "They are the remotest nation, the most just of men; the favorites of the gods. The lofty inhabitants of Olympus journey to them, and take part in their feasts; their sacrifices are the most agreeable of all that mortals can offer them."

Nubia's geographical location, it seems, has had everything to do with its singular place in history. For generation upon generation, Nubians served as middlemen in a flourishing trade that linked Egypt with the raw wealth of Africa's tropical interior: gold and other precious metals, ivory, amethyst and ebony, incense, ostrich eggs and feathers, wild animals and their skins.

Central to the Nubian landscape—and fundamental in its role in Nubian history—is the Nile, the world's longest river. From its source in the highlands bordering the Great Rift Valley, the Nile streams north for more than 4,000 miles to the Mediterranean Sea, passing over alternating beds of sandstone and granite. Where it meets soft sandstone, the river broadens and its current flows unimpeded. But where it encounters unyielding granite, rocky outcrops and narrow canyons squeeze its waters to a raging torrent, creating a cataract. There are six cataracts—numbered from north to south—between Aswan in Egypt and present-day Khartoum, capital of the Sudan. Between them stretch regions of contrasting terrain, each of which has played a different role in the age-old Nubian drama.

The first and second cataracts defined the limits of Lower Nubia. In the area of the second cataract—a run of tumbling rapids—lay the Batn el Hagar, or Belly of Rocks. Here was the most forbidding of all Nubian terrain: a miles-long lunar landscape, strewn

Stretching southward from near modern Aswan, Egypt, to Khartoum, in the Sudan, ancient Nubia centered roughly around the meandering Nile River. Nubian civilizations were sustained by the waters of the Nile as well as by the many trade routes that traversed the region.

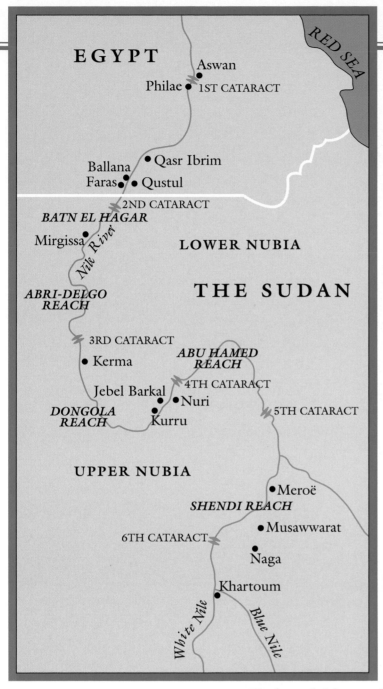

with boulders and inimical to settlement. For a thousand years after the rise of dynastic Egypt, the second cataract posed an impenetrable barrier to the pharaohs' conquering armies.

Between the third and fourth cataracts extended the Dongola Reach, a wide, well-watered, heavily cultivated plain that made up the heartland of the ancient kingdom of Kush. Marking the southern limit of Nubia was the sixth cataract north of Khartoum, where the Blue and White Niles converge. To its north, extending nearly as far as the fifth cataract, were the bountiful plains of the Shendi Reach, home of the latter-day Nubian kingdom of Meroë.

The Greek historian Diodorus Siculus inaccurately, but reverently, called this vast stretch of nearly 1,000 miles (from the first cataract to the sixth) the fountainhead of Egypt's civilization, but the Western world paid little attention to ancient Nubia past the classical age. Not until the 19th century did this ancient land reclaim the attention of Western scholars. The indirect cause of renewed interest was the conquest of the Sudan, in which most of Nubia's territory lay. In 1820 the Turkish viceroy of Egypt, Muhammad Ali Pasha, bent on enlarging his empire, dispatched an army of 4,000 men to the south. With them went a small band of European adventurers eager to rediscover the legendary Nubian kingdoms of Kush and Meroë. Their explorations resulted in several evocative books and drawings that served to stimulate public and scientific interest in this corner of the world *(pages 20-21)*.

One of the more colorful participants in the Nubian revival was the American Bayard Taylor, an acclaimed journalist and poet, whose visit resulted in a book, *Life and Landscapes from Egypt to the Negro Kingdoms of the White Nile*. It would become an invaluable guide to the ruins of ancient Kush. Unfortunately, it would also perpetuate the ignorant but broadly held notion that all of the region's splendid monuments were the work either of Egyptians or of Indian

19

A SCHOLAR AMONG MERCENARIES

The viceroy of Egypt, Muhammad Ali Pasha, certainly did not have archaeology in mind when he sent 4,000 troops up the Nile from Cairo in July 1820. Hoping to form what one historian called the "black army of his dreams," he hungered for slaves—and for the gold mines said to lie almost 2,000 miles away at Fazughli, a village on the Blue Nile near the Ethiopian border. And he had few qualms about using force to obtain his goals: He offered money for each ear taken in battle,

and his soldiers delivered some 3,000—severed from the living as well as the dead—after a bloody massacre in November.

Yet Muhammad Ali's campaign of conquest added much to scholars' understanding of the Upper Nile, for he permitted the French mineralogist and geologist Frédéric Cailliaud to travel along in exchange for prospecting help. Cailliaud and his traveling companion, Pierre Letorzec, thus became among the very first Europeans since antiquity to eye such sites as

the Meroë pyramids of Nubia (*background*), which Cailliaud recorded with an archaeologist's curiosity and an artist's skill. His maps and drawings, two of which are at right, became the basis for all subsequent excavations at Meroë.

Cailliaud stands atop the pyramid at far right in this engraving of Meroë from his 1826 account of his trip up the Nile. Subsequent explorers discovered that he carved his name into the wall of a chapel, several of which can be seen in front of the pyramids.

Cailliaud, dressed in Turkish garb in order to keep from offending his hosts, sketches near a 13-foot-tall granite colossus at the quarries of Dongola, about 45 miles south of the Nile's third cataract, while his friend Letorzec smokes a long pipe.

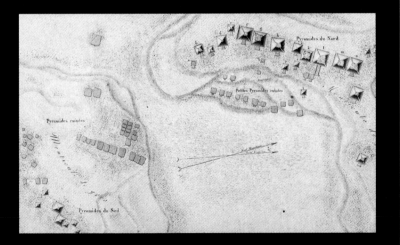

A pair of arrows at the center of Cailliaud's map of the Meroë pyramids point toward true and magnetic north. The explorers and camels rendered at left are approaching the group of pyramids marked with the letters A through X (upper right).

or Arab emigrants. In any case, said Taylor, the structures had surely been built by "an offshoot of the race to which we belong."

As would happen a few years later when Mauch and Bent reached Great Zimbabwe, the sum total of a black African culture's achievements were being ascribed to another race. And, as with Great Zimbabwe, archaeology would prove the key to unfettering Nubia's past from the bonds of prejudice.

To be sure, there are conspicuous signs of Egyptian influence throughout Nubian history. Egypt dominated Lower Nubia militarily for centuries. But despite the constant friction and frequent clashes, Nubians clearly venerated many of their more cosmopolitan neighbor's customs. Even during the height of Nubian power, when the Kingdom of Kush conquered Egypt and established its own pharaonic dynasty, which lasted 60 years, Nubian rulers emulated their Egyptian predecessors in dress and manner. Nevertheless, Nubia had always had a thriving culture in its own right. As has happened with countless cultures on every continent, Nubians merely incorporated foreign—in this case Egyptian—elements that they admired in order to enrich their own traditions.

The herculean task of piecing together the splintered history of Nubia did not begin in earnest until the first quarter of the 20th century. In 1906, in an effort to expand the irrigation and hydroelectric potential of the Nile, the Egyptian government announced plans to raise the level of the Aswan Dam—forerunner of the well-known Aswan High Dam built in the 1960s—by some 17 feet. When the resultant floodwaters threatened to inundate a vast stretch of unexcavated Nubian treasures, Egyptian officials recruited the

So thin-walled that they are described as "egg-shell" pottery, vessels such as these delicate clay pots are characteristic of the so-called A-group Nubian culture, which peaked about 3000 BC. The vessel at left is painted in red with a basket-weave design; the other was patterned with fingerprints of the artisan who made it.

American archaeologist George Andrew Reisner to head up what was officially designated the First Archaeological Survey of Nubia.

Between 1907 and 1911 Reisner—a curator of the Boston Museum of Fine Arts renowned for his prior work at the great pyramids of Giza—undertook the systematic excavation of 95 miles of Lower Nubian territory. The massive salvage operation unearthed 151 cemeteries, with some 8,000 burials. From a study of the grave goods, Reisner distinguished different and distinct groups—the product of migration and shifting populations, he believed. Later archaeological research, however, has unearthed evidence indicating a much greater degree of cultural continuity than Reisner suspected.

Lacking written records or any indication of what these peoples called themselves, Reisner rather unpoetically assigned alphabetical titles, such as A-group and C-group. The appearance of the seminomadic A-group around 3800 BC marks the sprouting of the seed that would later emerge as a distinct civilization. In the graves of these early peoples—well preserved by the arid climate—Reisner detected the first evidence of wealth and ritual belief.

The dead were interred in oval or rectangular pits capped with courses of undressed stones. Inside, desiccated bodies lay on their sides in a contracted position, with the head facing west. Corpses were dressed in linen or long, fringed leather kilts and swaddled in straw matting and halfa grass. Many wore necklaces, pendants, and amulets, variously fashioned from shell, bone, ivory, stone, or blue-green faience. Feathers and leather caps adorned their heads.

A-group graves of both sexes contained pebbles and quartzite palettes used for grinding and mixing the green malachite eye paint then stylish in both Egypt and Nubia. Often, tiny clay figurines of people and animals kept watch over the deceased, next to baskets, filled with seeds and fruit remains, and lovely, thin-walled pottery washed in red ochre and decorated with geometric designs. A few graves were extraordinary for their richness. One contained a number of heavy copper axes, a lion's head of rose quartz overlaid with glaze, a mica mirror, and two ceremonial maces with gilded handles, around which a row of animals march in low relief.

Since the majority of these objects came from Egypt, scholars have surmised that they were presents bestowed by Egyptian trading partners upon prominent A-group personages—perhaps chiefs or kings. Copper axes of an Egyptian type unearthed in the graves of many lesser individuals, along with Egyptian beer and

wine jars, further
suggest a trade rela-
tionship between the
Nubians and the Egyp-
tians. The A-group proba-
bly received such luxuries in
exchange for acting as middlemen in the shipment of tropical trade goods, such as ivory, to
the Egyptian emporium at Aswan.

In later years, the quality and
quantity of Egyptian exports in A-group graves show a marked decline. Apparently, with the unification of Upper and Lower Egypt
under one ruler around 3100 BC, the fortunes of the A-group
waned. During this early period of dynastic rule, known as the Old
Kingdom, a united, powerful Egypt could seize from Nubia what it
had once obtained through barter. A third-millennium BC Egyptian
engraving on a rock near the second cataract graphically portrays this
change. A Nubian chief is shown bound to the prow of an Egyptian
ship, while the bodies of the vanquished float alongside. The relief
depicts the victory of Egyptian king Djer over two A-group villages.

Due, perhaps, to such aggression, almost all traces of A-group
culture disappear from the archaeological record by the early third
millennium BC. An interval of six centuries elapsed, during which
Lower Nubia seems to have been virtually uninhabited except for

Testimony to the frequently close links between ancient Egypt and Nubia, this detailed model of a company of dark-skinned Nubian archers was found standing next to a similar troop of lighter-skinned Egyptian spearmen in an Egyptian tomb dating to about 2100 BC.

A drawing of a relief—dating from 3100 to 2900 BC—carved on a rock near the second cataract apparently commemorates a successful Egyptian raid into Nubia. One captive stands with hands bound behind his back, while another is tied to the prow of an Egyptian ship sailing past the bodies of four drowned Nubians.

scattered bands of nomads. Then, quite abruptly around 2300 BC, a new culture appeared in the semiarid valley between the first and second cataracts. This was Reisner's C-group, a sedentary people whose burial practices and material goods imply strong ties with the vanished A-group. They, too, buried their dead—similarly dressed—in oval pits but piled dirt on top to create tumuluses. Later C-group grave sites included aboveground chapels to honor the deceased.

Etchings of long-horned cattle on pottery, rocks, and grave markers suggested to Reisner a preoccupation with livestock not shared by earlier Nubians. In later burials, Reisner found skeletons of sacrificial sheep, goats, gazelles, and dogs. In the richest tombs, clusters of cattle skulls decorated the chamber.

C-group graves also revealed considerable evidence of renewed trade with Egypt. Reisner discovered numerous seal amulets of Old Kingdom vintage, along with Egyptian round-bottomed pottery vessels for holding foodstuffs. Absent, however, were the cosmetic palettes so popular in A-group Nubia. Occasionally, a skeleton was found clutching an Egyptian copper mirror before its face.

During this period, Egyptian power was on the wane as the Old Kingdom grew weaker. Burial inscriptions adorning the tombs of the provincial governors of Aswan—those Egyptian officials charged with monitoring the southern trade—suggest that the earlier formula of trade with Nubia had supplanted extortion and seizure. Sometimes the Egyptians were forced to purchase the goodwill of C-group chiefs to gain safe passage for their agents journeying south to obtain cattle, timber, and mercenaries for the Egyptian army.

The most famous of these postmortem accounts emblazoned the tomb of Harkhuf, governor of Aswan under the child pharaoh Pepy II. Harkhuf led several eight-month expeditions through Lower Nubia to the mysterious southern kingdom that the Egyptians called Yam, traveling overland by donkey caravan to avoid the second cataract. On his third trip, the governor reportedly returned with 300 donkeys laden with leopard skins, elephant tusks, ebony, incense, and oil. A troop of newly recruited Yamite mercenaries accompanied Harkhuf, enabling him to pass through C-group territory unscathed. On his final journey to Yam, he bought a dancing dwarf to delight his young monarch.

The independence of the C-group Nubians remained unchallenged until around the beginning of the second millennium BC. By then the Egyptians had entered a new era of strength and prosperity known as the Middle Kingdom. Pharaohs Senusret I and III launched military campaigns that extended Egypt's control past the second cataract for the first time.

The Egyptians secured their new holdings with a series of

colossal mud-brick fortifications strategically positioned between the first and second cataracts. These bastions watched over both the subjected Nubian populace and the lucrative Nile trade. All goods destined for Egypt funneled through the largest of the forts, located at Mirgissa, near the second cataract.

Excavations conducted there by the French during the mid-1960s revealed a large mud slipway where boats could portage around the rapids. The dried mud still bore the imprints of boat keels and human feet. Inside the fort were found stone forms used to shape hide shields and quantities of wood for making shield handles. The flint points of more than 75 javelins and spears lay near the walls.

The extensive armory at Mirgissa reflects Egypt's wary regard for its southern neighbor. By the time of the Middle Kingdom, the C-group had given way to a more centralized and more powerful entity: the Kingdom of Kush, whose ruler resided beyond Egyptian reach at Kerma, south of the third cataract in the fertile Dongola Reach. In all probability, many archaeologists say, Yam and Kush were one and the same, known by different names at different times. But while Yam seems to have enjoyed a friendly trading relationship with Egypt, Kush was regarded with fear and scorn. Small clay tablets excavated at several of the Middle Kingdom forts bore the words *Kush* or *Ruler of Kush;* each had been deliberately smashed in an attempt to magically weaken the southern kingdom.

In the late 17th century BC, Egypt faced an even greater threat from the north: Invaders from Palestine known as Hyksos swept into the delta region and wrested power from the pharaoh, who fled south to Thebes. Considerably weakened, Egypt abandoned its second cataract fortresses and withdrew north to Aswan, leaving Lower Nubia without an overlord for the first time in 300 years. The Kingdom of Kush wasted no time in filling the power vacuum. At Mirgissa, close to the towering walls of the Egyptian fortress, archaeologists discovered a cemetery containing the graves of 22 Kerma warriors. Many other Kerma-style graves have been found throughout Lower Nubia, mostly near the great Egyptian fortresses and all dating to the period of Hyksos domination of northern Egypt. Archaeologists conclude that the ruler of Kerma had garrisoned troops in the former Egyptian strongholds and set himself up as master of the region, prompting a Theban dynast to lament: "I sit united with an Asiatic and a Nubian, each man in possession of his slice of this Egypt."

Shown against a scale model of the Nubian town of Kerma, first capital of the Kingdom of Kush, the 4,000-year-old ruins of the Western Defuffa stand as a monument to early Nubian religious beliefs. Made of unbaked brick, the building is thought to have been Kerma's principal religious structure and can be seen at top center in the model.

With the occupation of Lower Nubia, Kerma entered its golden age. Now firmly in control of the profitable southern trade routes, the kingdom conducted commerce with the Egyptian north on quite favorable terms, growing enormously rich on the proceeds. The opulence of this time is clearly reflected in the cemetery adjoining the town of Kerma, first excavated by Reisner in 1913. He identified thousands of graves, but eight in particular proved fascinating. They were covered by circular earthen mounds of enormous proportions, the largest as long as a football field.

Each mound enclosed a spacious burial chamber—larger than those inside the great pyramids. In the chamber, the corpse of an obviously high-ranking personage reclined on an *angareeb*—the four-legged bed, made of woven rope or split palm ribs stretched over a wooden frame, that is characteristic of Kushite burials. The bed was strewn with gold and surrounded by beautifully crafted objects of bronze, ivory, and faience.

But this scene of peaceful repose contrasted chillingly with the larger view inside the mounds. Within corridors of mud-brick walls adjoining the burial chambers lay the contorted bodies of hundreds of men, women, and children. In one tomb, Reisner counted 322 victims—the largest number of human sacrifices ever found in a single burial anywhere in the world. From the positions of the bodies, he deduced that they had been buried alive.

In his 1923 book, *Excavations at Kerma*, Reisner conjures up the scene at such a funeral: "They proceed, not in the ceremonial silence of our funerals, but with all the 'ululations' and wailings of the people of the Nile." After the bed with the body has been placed inside, "the doors of the chambers are closed and sealed. The priests and officials withdraw. The women and attendants take their places jostling in the narrow corridor. The cries and all movements cease. The signal is given. The crowd of people assembled for the feast, now waiting ready, cast the earth from their baskets upon the still, but living victims on the floor and rush away for more. The emotions of the victims may perhaps be exaggerated by ourselves, they were for-

Cattle horns—remains of animals that were sacrificed at an 18th-century BC royal funeral—festoon the rim of a tomb in Kerma. Later royal graves at the same site contained dozens, even hundreds, of human sacrifices.

Preserved by the dry climate, the body of a young Kerma archer of the 18th century BC reposes on a leather mat, his hand still gripping a bowstring; the remains of a quiver, arrows, and a bow were found nearby. Bespeaking a warrior culture, weapons—such as this bronze dagger (inset) found on the hip of an infant's skeleton—are common in Kerma graves.

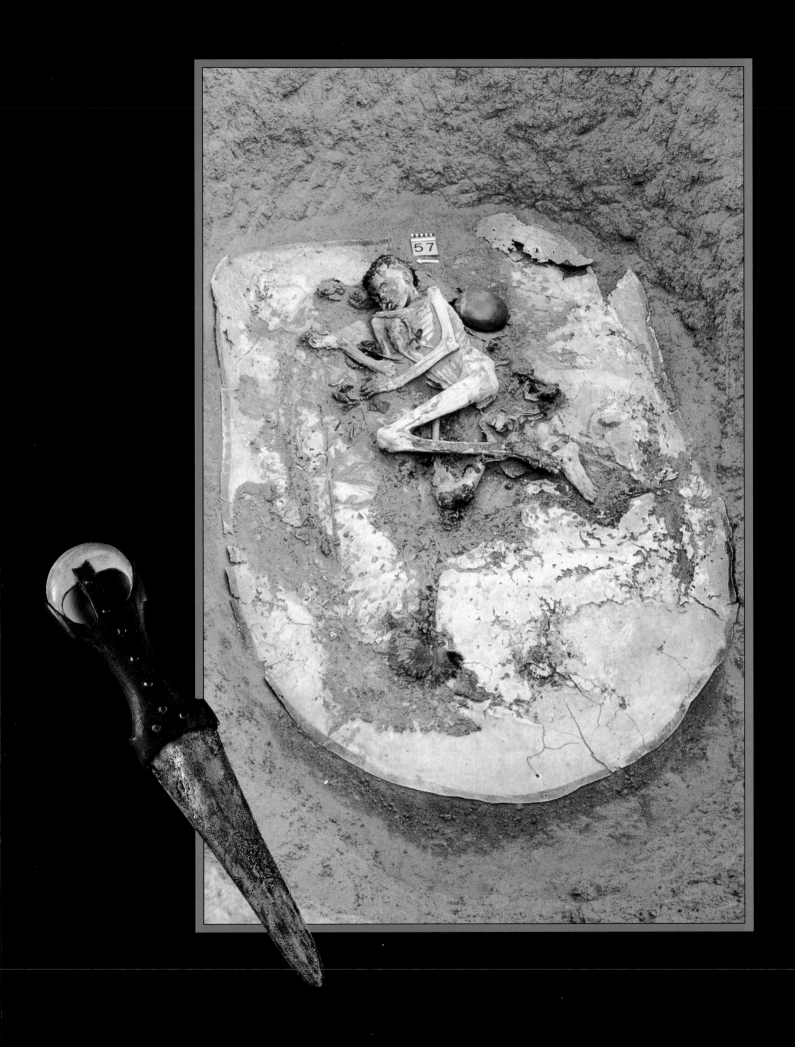

tified by their religious beliefs and had taken their places willingly without a doubt, but at that last moment, we know from their attitudes in death that a rustle of fear passed through them and that in some cases there was a spasm of physical agony."

On a less somber tone, Reisner also explored a massive mudbrick building called the Western Defuffa *(page 26)*, two miles from the cemetery. A towering structure once considerably taller than its present-day height of 60 feet, the Defuffa had a solid masonry interior pierced by a single staircase. Adjoining the Defuffa's western face were several brick rooms containing the broken fragments of Egyptian objects, including alabaster ointment jars, faience and stone vessels, beads, crystals, and bits of bronze. Reisner also identified 565 impressions of Egyptian mud seals that had once been affixed to pots and baskets, and a large assortment of raw materials, such as lumps of resin and blocks of mica, that had been used in assembling and finishing trade goods. From the finds Reisner deduced that the Western Defuffa had functioned as a combination factory and warehouse for items in the Nile trade.

However, more recent excavations by Charles Bonnet of the University of Geneva suggest that, earlier on, the Defuffa had been a temple. A small internal passageway may have served as the sanctuary; in front of it stood a circular limestone altar most likely used for animal sacrifice. A staircase once led to a rooftop terrace, where priests may have conducted ceremonies of some kind.

According to Bonnet, the Western Defuffa constituted the spiritual and physical center of the ancient town of Kerma. From humble beginnings in the late fourth millennium BC, Kerma rose to become, by its heyday during the early 16th century BC, a 25-acre walled town with a population of 2,000. Artisans, priests, bureaucrats, traders, and farmers dwelled in its comfortable houses of mud brick or wood, each with a courtyard to shelter livestock. Ringing the perimeter was a network of dry ditches and mud-brick walls.

Formidable though they were, Kerma's defenses did not hold indefinitely. By the late 16th century BC, the reinvigorated Theban pharaohs had ousted the Hyksos from the delta region and launched a military campaign to reclaim Egypt's lost lands. After routing the foreign invaders, the pharaoh Ahmose turned his attentions southward. In what is known as the Great Annihilation, his army laid waste Upper Nubia's fertile plains, burning crops and granaries and razing straw huts and stone dwellings in its path. Upon reaching Kerma, the soldiers scaled the ancient ramparts and torched the town. The once-bustling trading emporium was leveled, and the Western Defuffa defiled. Signs of the wide-scale burning and destruction can still be read in the charred courses of Kerma's massive walls.

Fifty years later, the pharaoh Thutmose I sailed south with his armada along the Nile's tortured course, intent on extinguishing the troublesome Kushites forever. Successfully navigating the steep, ascending rapids of the fourth cataract for the first time, Thutmose I established a new Egyptian frontier at the Abu Hamed Reach. Perhaps in emulation of the Old Kingdom rock engraving at the second cataract, he returned to Thebes with a Kerma warrior tied to his ship's prow. A successor, Thutmose III, formally annexed all of the Nubian lands north of the fourth cataract, effectively dissolving the Kingdom of Kush for good.

Egypt's domination of Nubia would endure for another 500 years. During those five centuries, the upper classes of Nubian society became thoroughly acculturated, as they adopted Egyptian dress, theology, and funerary practices. Yet, beneath their borrowed personas, the people of Nubia retained an impassioned sense of their own cultural identity. The tenacious quality of their spirit would ultimately lead the Nubians to challenge—and to conquer—their Egyptian rivals, giving rise to the greatest and most sophisticated of Nubia's civilizations, the Kingdoms of Napata and Meroë.

JOURNEY IN SEARCH OF NUBIA

Upon completion of his second expedition to Nubia between 1906 and 1907, the American archaeologist James H. Breasted *(above, right)* expressed "great satisfaction to be carrying away—for the first time it has ever been done—as much of the record of an entire age and people as has survived in the wreckage of a great kingdom." What Breasted, a professor of Egyptology with the University of Chicago, carried away from this region of the Middle Nile was a photographic survey of ancient monuments considered the finest archive of Nubian architecture and inscriptions in existence. Traveling up the Nile by feluccas (the small Egyptian sailboats shown in the background) and across the desert by camel, Breasted, photographer Horst Schliephack, and Egyptologist Norman de Garis Davies visited numerous sites they believed to be outposts of Egyptian culture. Due in part to the men's scrupulous documentation, the ruined pyramids, temples, and palaces the team photographed are now known to be the religious and administrative centers of the independent kingdom of Kush.

In a series of journals (one of which is shown above, left), Professor Breasted recorded, day by day, the adventures and difficulties the three men faced while attempting to procure the nearly 1,100 images they eventually sent back to Chicago, some of which are used to illustrate this picture essay. "Our first practical problem here has been sterilized water," the diarist grumbled. "Even when strained, it is so full of mud as to be almost unusable for photography. We filter and boil it for drinking, but after it has sizzled and been churned all day under a broiling sun on a camel's back the taste is disgusting."

Prodigious quantities of dust, grasshoppers, bats, and gnats contributed further to the expedition's difficulties. But the intrepid professor endured adverse circumstances with equanimity and humor. "Grasshopper in the soup tonight," Breasted noted offhandedly in his journal. "Of course he was served to me! I crunched on him for some time, supposing he was a piece of dried herb. But finding him invulnerable, I pulled him out, still intact, but very dead!"

Photographer Horst Schliephack sets up a shot atop a pyramid at Meroë, one-time capital of Kush. Though only in his thirties, Schliephack was a seasoned veteran, and despite blinding sandstorms and temperatures approaching 135°F, he produced outstanding images of the monuments on 8 x 10 glass plates. Breasted himself probably recorded this moment with the expedition's small roll-film camera.

Laden with supplies for the five-month expedition, camels trek through the desert to Nubian sites located inland from the Nile. Travel by caravan was slow going— a day's journey covered only 15 miles.

"Here we are at the pyramids of Meroë with nothing to live in!" wrote Breasted of his arrival at the first site on the itinerary, having been persuaded to leave his tents behind. "Finally I moved into the chapel of one pyramid, and Davies into the next," he continued. "Schliephack sleeps in his dark-room." Once settled, the men set to work, making a plan of the monuments they wished to record.

Meroë, the last capital and one of the largest cities of ancient Nubia, boasted a palace, government buildings, temples, and cemeteries for both commoners and nobility. Most interesting to the team, though, was the royal cemetery, built along the ridges to the east of the city, with more than 50 distinctive, stepped pyramids, several of which appear in the background photograph. The stone structures memorialized the rulers of Meroë, whose bodies were interred beneath them. Nubian pyramids differed from Egypt's, possessing steeply sloping sides and built-in chapels that were decorated with reliefs and inscriptions. Breasted wrote of one relief, "I wake every morning with a fat monarch, some relative of [the] queen whose capital this place was, looking benignly down upon me, as he waves the palm branch he has been holding for over 2,000 years."

Having scrambled up the dangerously dilapidated side of a royal tomb, two expedition members perch on its summit to photograph from a bird's-eye view some of Meroë's other pyramids. Archaeologists believe that Nubian pyramids—which measure from 18 to 90 feet high—were designed with a flat top, on which a finial or a statue stood.

Carved reliefs depicting processions of Nubians bearing offerings embellish the entrance to a mortuary chapel attached to the pyramid tomb of a queen of Meroë. Chapels, built on the eastern face of most royal pyramids, provided a sacred place for priests to hold ceremonies for the dead.

Traveling 50 miles into the desert by train and camel caravan, the expedition moved on to Naga, a large town belonging to the Meroitic kingdom. Naga's seven elaborately decorated and well-constructed stone temples mark it as an important religious center. Working at breakneck speed, the team photographed five of the temples in two days before setting out for Musawwarat es-Sufra, 10 miles to the north. There, the team found a vast, walled complex unlike any other in Nubia or Egypt. A temple sat at its center, its colonnade in ruins *(background)*, surrounded by open plazas and compounds connected by corridors and ramps.

"It is of imposing proportions [with] rich and ornate columns," wrote James Breasted in his description of the structure, which is known today as the Great Enclosure. "The masonry is of the finest character, in a white sandstone which weathers red. There has never been a large camera in these walls, and I soon had Schliephack at work, exposing plate after plate upon this fascinating place."

Adorned with the carved figures of a king and a queen, the facade of the temple at Naga (below) evokes its former grandeur. Although many facets of Nubian religion came from the Egyptians, this temple was dedicated to the local deity, Apedemak, a lion-headed god of war and abundance.

Stylized whorls representing wool cover a stone ram lying at the entrance to the Great Temple of Amen at Naga. The Nubians of Naga honored Amen, an Egyptian divinity often portrayed as a ram, with the building of an Egyptian-style, multiroomed temple.

Back on the Nile, Breasted traveled downriver to another of Kush's capital cities, Jebel Barkal, nestled at the foot of the sacred mountain for which it was named. From the vantage point of the summit, Horst Schliephack captured Jebel Barkal's pyramids against the sky *(below)*.

Since the beginning of the expedition, Professor Breasted had observed with growing dismay the wanton destruction of the Nubian monuments by foreigners in the name of archaeology or by locals for raw materials. At Jebel Barkal, he witnessed the use of ancient temple masonry blocks for a new burial and lamented, "I presume the mounds of this cemetery cover hundreds of inscribed stones which have thus disappeared."

Joined by Breasted's wife and young son, the team resumed its river journey, navigating perilous cataracts, almost losing the precious glass plates in one mishap, yet continuing to photograph sites along the way. By the time they reached their final destination, the members of the expedition had covered a thousand miles, compiling a visual history of inestimable value.

Wearing a late-Egyptian-style crown adorned with double serpents, the beautifully sculpted granite head of a Nubian king lies fallen in the rocky sand of Jebel Barkal. When reunited with its torso, found nearby, the statue stood more than 18 feet tall.

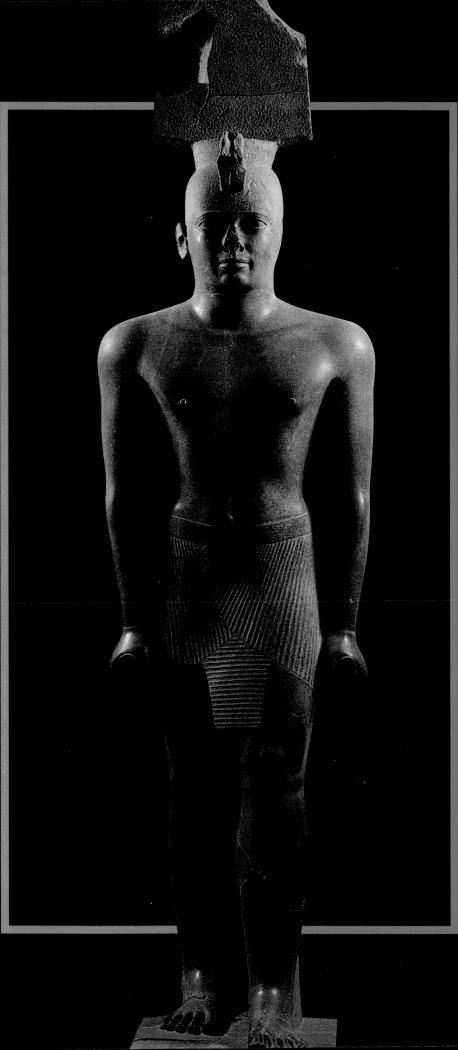

THE NUBIANS' ASCENT TO GREATNESS

The Nubian king Taharqa radiates power in this colossal statue from the temple complex at Jebel Barkal in the Sudan. As third pharaoh of the 25th Dynasty, Taharqa ruled not only Kush, as Nubia is known in the Bible, but also Egypt.

October 18, 1963, was a sad day for the women of the Egyptian village of Dabou. With the sun's first rays gilding the waters of the Nile, they made their way solemnly to the cemetery that housed the graves of their loved ones and ancestors. In a traditional gesture of benediction, they sprinkled water over the tombs and departed in silence, choked with grief, for they knew this place was lost to them forever. They then rejoined their families, gathered up their bundled belongings, and went down to board the boats that would carry them into unwelcome exile. At the moment of departure, some people kissed the soil they had farmed for so long, while others scooped up a handful of earth to carry with them.

The same scene was repeated in dozens of villages up and down the river, between the first and third cataracts of the Nile, in the 300-mile-long stretch of southern Egypt and northern Sudan that had once been part of the ancient land of Nubia. Bowing to the will of their governments, and accepting that the circumstances were beyond their control, 100,000 Nubians faced loss of their ancestral lands and relocation to new settlements elsewhere. "As we were sailing," reflected one emigrant, "I recalled Noah's ark. The boat was crowded, filled with personal belongings, poultry, animals, and pets. We were all heading toward the unknown." The cause of the Nubians' exodus was the impending construction of the huge dam

and reservoir on the Nile that would put their homes at the bottom of a vast artificial lake.

The Egyptian government had decided to undertake this massive project, with all its far-reaching human and environmental implications, in response to demographers' warnings of a looming population explosion on a potentially catastrophic scale. The nation's natural resources were already seriously overextended. Leaders warned of famine and economic chaos if the country's agricultural and industrial productivity were not rapidly and radically improved.

To forestall such a disaster, the Egyptians turned, as they had for millennia, to their perpetual life source, the Nile River. The ancient pharaohs built flood-control canals, and in 1902 their 20th-century successors erected a dam at Aswan, 250 miles north of the modern Sudanese border. This first Aswan dam resulted in temporary seasonal flooding of an area south of Aswan, site of the Philae temple complex, as well as a portion of ancient Nubia, with some areas submerged for up to six months of the year. But the new Aswan High Dam posed a much greater threat; it promised to engulf permanently a large tract of Nubian land. The two-mile-long barrier would nearly double the previous high-water level of the Nile and

Feluccas ply the waters of the Nile around Philae and its temple complex in this oil painting by Scottish artist and traveler David Roberts. He visited the Egyptian island in 1838, six decades before work began on the first Aswan dam, precursor to the Aswan High Dam. The original barrier, completed in 1902 and twice heightened, caused periodic flooding of Philae.

create a lake 300 miles long and six miles wide. The project's engineers sought to prevent the devastating floods caused when the river's annual inundation was more abundant than usual, while providing storage of sufficient water for unexpected dry periods. The dam also would increase Egypt's capability to produce cheap hydroelectric power for industrial development.

But with these gains came tragic losses. The plan affected all the villages in Egyptian Nubia and almost one-third of those in the Sudan. The Egyptians were moved to new settlements in the Kom Ombo region, still within the region of Aswan but in a landscape devoid of palm groves, dunes, rocky hills, and the people's beloved Nile. Even more radically, Sudanese Nubians were resettled in an area located nearly 500 miles away from their former homes, close to the Ethiopian border, with a climate and soil so different that the newcomers would have to learn new farming methods in order to survive. In addition, all Nubians stood to lose their own history as a priceless legacy of ancient temples, tombs, and monuments vanished forever beneath the waters.

In the Middle Nile Valley, its land long shaped by the river and defined by the rhythm of its floods, settlement patterns had changed little over the millennia, and relics of Nubia's earliest inhabitants remained. Apart from the Dongola Reach, a fertile plain formed by a bend in the river, there were only narrow strips of cultivable land along the bank, separated by stretches of sandstone cliffs, or scattered islands green with vegetation affording a little space for crops. In the rocky environs of the cataracts, the terrain was strewn with granite boulders and almost impossible to farm. Still, this hot, arid, starkly beautiful, and seemingly inhospitable land was home to a prodigiously gifted people.

Early Egyptians knew Nubia by various names, including Ta-Seti (Land of the Bow), Yam, and Wawat. Later Egyptian chronicles and the Bible called it Kush. Ancient historians knew Kush as the nation that conquered Egypt in the eighth century BC and ruled it for 60 years. Greeks and Romans labeled it Aethiopia, or "Land of Burnt Faces," a name which, in modern times, applies to the country farther south that ancient geographers dubbed Abyssinia. Classical authors wrote imaginatively of the brilliant "Aethiopian" kingdom of Meroë, and foreign merchants clamored for its incense, ivory, ebony, and gold. Pilgrims from many lands visited its celebrated shrines. When Western scholars rediscovered the all-but-forgotten

43

ancient cities of Nubia in the 19th century, most seemed incapable of acknowledging them as the creation of Africans, suggesting instead that they had been built by foreign settlers.

By the 20th century, some students of the region began to explore its past, but Nubia's isolation kept major excavations to a minimum. Now, when much of Nubia faced virtual eradication, archaeologists began to apprehend the value of what they were about to lose. Here, in the 11th hour, this narrow corridor between the Mediterranean world and the African interior rapidly revealed itself as a rich repository of 6,000 years of human experience and creativity, extending from the Paleolithic era of prehistory to the modern age.

The international scientific community signaled its alarm. Archaeological landmarks of incalculable importance, such as the great rock-cut memorial at Abu Simbel that the pharaoh Ramses II commissioned to impress the Nubians with Egyptian power, lay within the territory destined for submersion. So, too, did many still-unexcavated sites, full of material treasures and vital information about the ancient civilizations along the Nile. Indeed, archaeologists began to conclude that the whole of Nubia was, in the words of one of their number, "the greatest open-air museum in the world."

But the juggernaut of economic pressures proved unstoppable. Both Egypt and its even poorer neighbor Sudan, a country that would see little direct benefit from these downstream developments, agonized but agreed that there was no alternative to the dam. The two states turned to the United Nations for help. Inaugurating a campaign for funds, Vittorino Veronese, director general of the United Nations Educational, Scientific, and Cultural Organization (UNESCO), announced that the two governments concerned were throwing open the affected territo-

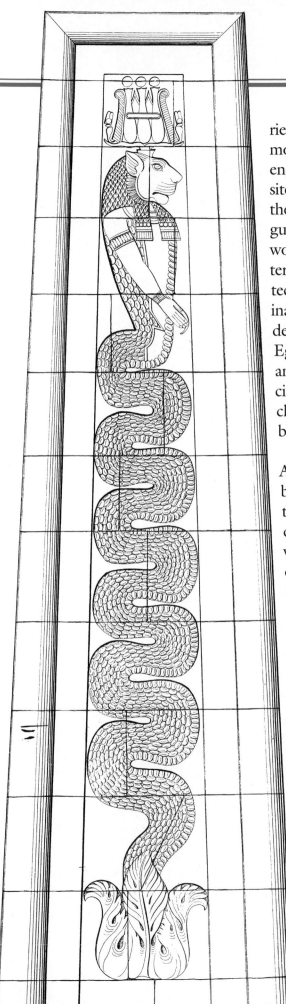

Apedemak, Meroitic god of war and abundance, takes the combined form of lion, human, and serpent in this drawing of a pylon from a temple that King Natakamani and Queen Amanitore built at Naga, located about 80 miles northeast of Khartoum in the Butana desert.

ries for intensive archaeological excavation and study. When possible, monuments would be transferred, by heroic and expensive feats of engineering, to the safety of higher ground or even to overseas sites (such as New York City's Metropolitan Museum of Art, where the Temple of Dendur, built in Nubia by the Roman emperor Augustus, is now housed). Those structures that could not be moved would be meticulously scrutinized, analyzed, and recorded for posterity by teams of archaeologists, photographers, surveyors, architects, designers, copyists, and experts in ancient languages. The originals themselves might be flooded over, but their images, and every detail of their construction and appearance, would survive. The Egyptian government already had established the Documentation and Study Center for the History of the Art and Civilization of Ancient Egypt to train new specialists and provide an archive for the architectural drawings and copied texts. The solution was not ideal, but it seemed to be the only option.

In January 1960 work started on the construction of the Aswan High Dam, while excavation teams from all over the world began arriving in Nubia to join forces with their colleagues from the Egyptian and Sudanese Antiquities Services. Crews and individual experts from more than 20 different nations set to work along the Nile, well aware that the dam builders were hard on their heels. They had barely five years to survey and study the whole of Lower Nubia, from the relatively well-documented sites within Egypt's boundaries to the hitherto uncharted stretches of the realm's northern reaches in the Sudan. The archaeological rescue operation was on.

The new arrivals set up their base camps in temporary tent cities, on houseboats afloat on the river, or in village houses. Nubian villages frequently sat directly atop layers and layers of previous settlements and afforded the best starting point for excavations. Rex Keating, a UNESCO staff member, remembered a fortuitous accident that took place during a visit to the Scandinavian headquarters, billeted in a Nubian house: "We were enjoying the evening meal when, abruptly, my chair leg went through the top of an ancient tomb that lay unsuspected under the mud floor beneath the dining table." Expedition members, Keating went on to say, became accustomed to finding their Land Rovers bogged down in ditches and potholes that turned out to be long-forgotten graves.

The moving of the immense monuments at Abu Simbel to higher ground captured the attention of the international media, but there were other, equally dramatic salvage operations, notably that of the temple complex of Philae in Lower Nubia, at the head of the first cataract of the Nile, just south of Aswan. The site occupied a tiny island measuring no more than 500 yards long and 160 yards wide, crammed with colonnaded courts and walls, great pylons carved with images of gods and kings in scenes of war or sacrifice, columns crowned with delicately floral capitals, pink-granite lions, obelisks, altars, and sanctuaries.

Yet Philae's relatively small compass in no way reflected its far-reaching historical, theological, and political significance. In the third century BC, the islet emerged as an important center of worship for the fertility goddess Isis. For thousands of years, the goddess figured prominently in the Egyptian pantheon, but during the period when the last native Egyptian pharaohs had been supplanted by the Ptolemaic Greeks, Isis became the focus of a truly international cult. Nubians, Egyptians, Greeks, Romans, and desert nomads all revered her and made Philae, which they called the Holy Island and the Interior of Heaven, a place of pilgrimage.

Philae's temple walls bore the marks of its multiethnic devotees. Official inscriptions by priests or royal benefactors mingled with many centuries of graffiti written in a babel of tongues and scripts, including Egyptian, Greek, Latin, Coptic, and Meroitic, the still undeciphered language of the great Nubian kingdom of Meroë *(page 44)*, which flourished from about 300 BC to AD 350. A Nubian prince, writing in hieratic, or cursive, Egyptian, prayed to Isis for protection on his return home, asking, "Oh my lady, you who distribute lands to the gods, see to me that I be brought back to Meroë, the beautiful city of your beloved son." In an effort to stamp out all remaining vestiges of paganism, the Byzantine emperor Justinian ordered the shrine's closure in the sixth century AD. But, as Justinian's historian, Procopius, noted at the time, "The temples remained in romantic ruin for posterity to wonder at."

In 1873 the Victorian author and avid Egyptologist Amelia Edwards rhapsodized over the "perfect grace and exquisite beauty"

Crowned with a cow's horns and the sun disk, the goddess Hathor suckles Queen Nefru-ka-Kashta, a wife of Piye, in a two-inch gilt silver amulet from the royal tombs at El Kurru, near Jebel Barkal. In Egypt, kings had been traditionally shown suckling at the goddess's breasts. This image of a queen doing so was unique to Kush.

A Nubian treasure, the eighth-century BC rock-crystal ball amulet at right, once worn on a necklace by a Kushite queen, is adorned with Hathor, a goddess associated with female sexuality, foreign lands, and exotic stones and substances. The hollow, cylindrical shaft visible with-in the orb likely served as a container for some charmed substance.

of Philae. "The approach by water is quite the most beautiful," she wrote. "Seen from the level of a small boat, the island, with its palms, its colonnades, its pylons, seems to rise out of the river like a mirage. Piled rocks frame it on either side, and the purple mountains close up the distance. As the boat glides nearer between glistening boulders, those sculptured towers rise higher and even higher against the sky. They show no sign of ruin or age. All looks solid, stately, perfect. One forgets for the moment that anything is changed. If a sound of antique chanting were to be borne along the quiet air—if a procession of white-robed priests bearing aloft the veiled ark of the God were to come sweeping round between the palms and pylons—we should not think it strange."

A scant quarter of a century after Edwards's visit, change in the name of progress nearly finished off what Justinian began. The building of the first Aswan dam at the start of the 20th century left the island flooded for most of the year. Only between July and October did the temples emerge from the water. Now, with the second dam about to drown the Holy Island once and for all, the international community considered various rescue strategies. Some experts suggested encircling Philae with a protective dam of its own. Others proposed that the temples should be temporarily dismantled, allowing new layers to be added to their original foundations, and then reerected, 26 feet higher than they were before. But these and other proposals foundered on technical, financial, and aesthetic grounds, and the specialists finally focused on the crucial issue of how best to respect what they deemed the "integrity of the monuments."

In the end, the experts chose the most daring scheme of all those that had been proposed. The buildings of Philae were to be dismantled, stone by stone, and transferred to the island of Agilkia, which, although only a quarter of a mile from Philae, would remain above the level of the reservoir. There, the temples of

Philae would be reconstructed in exactly the same positions they had occupied at their original site. Engineering work began in 1972, and on March 29, 1977, the first stone of the Temple of Isis was ceremoniously placed in its new location. By August of 1979 the rescue of Philae was complete.

However spectacular the feats of engineering, the archaeological rescue and salvage of Nubian monuments remained far more straightforward and far less painful than the transfer of the Nubians themselves. "We would be better looked after if we were statues" was an oft-heard remark among those compelled to leave the land that had been home to their ancestors since the days when the paint was still fresh on the walls of the Philae temples.

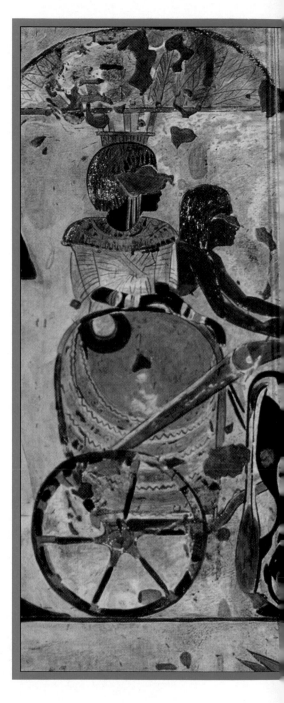

For thousands of years before the construction of the Aswan dams, Nubians had lived in the shadow of their more powerful northern neighbor. Until well into the first millennium BC, Egypt dominated Nubia economically and, for long periods, politically. The earliest images of Nubians appear in Egyptian wall paintings, delivering tribute to the pharaoh or one of his court officials. A tomb painting in Thebes features a procession of handsome young Nubian princes bearing exotic wild-animal skins, ivory, and, most interesting of all to the recipients, large rings of gold from Nubian mines.

The archaeological evidence from graves of the age suggests that the Nubians absorbed cultural and religious influences from their colonial overlords. In fact, princes of the Nubian royal family often were taken to Egypt to learn Egyptian ways. But although the Nubians worshiped many of the same gods and wore similar wigs and linen garments, in the eyes of the Egyptians the Nubians maintained their subject status. Egyptian writers seldom forgot, when referring to Kush, to apply such epithets as "miserable," "vile," and "defeated." Traditionally, the pharaoh wore sandals decorated on the soles with images of Nubians and Syrians to remind himself—and them— that he had crushed them underfoot.

In the eighth century BC, though, the tables turned. Egypt's rulers grew weak, and the kingdom split in two. The northern part fragmented into small, semiautonomous kingdoms, while the south followed the priests of the god Amen at Thebes. Aided and abetted by the Egyptian priests, a dynasty of Nubian kings came to see themselves as the only fitting inheritors to the pharaoh's throne. Around

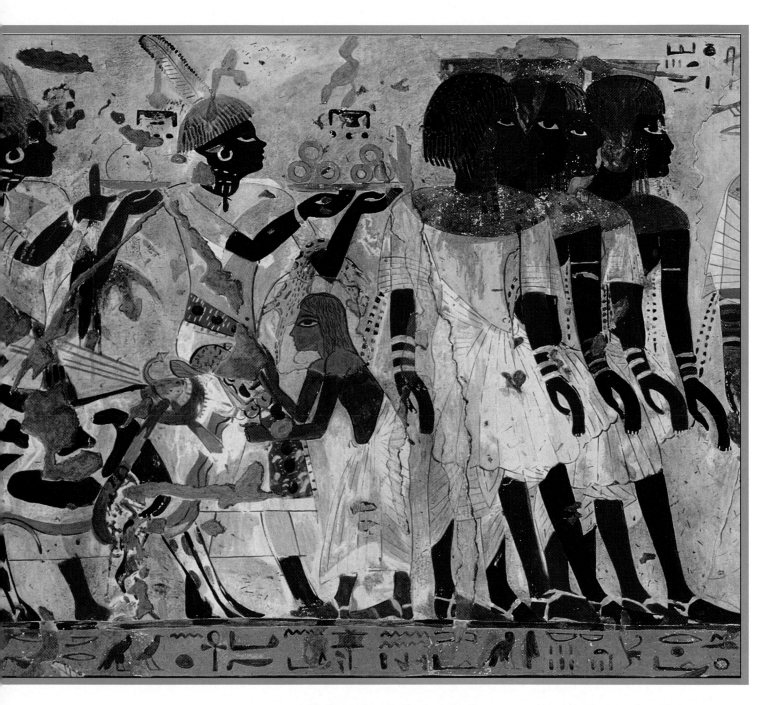

A Nubian princess rides in a chariot drawn by two oxen, while members of her retinue carry gold rings, leopard pelts, and other gifts for the pharaoh Tutankhamen on behalf of his viceroy in Kush, Huy. The scene is part of a wall painting *found in Huy's tomb at Thebes, portraying his investiture as "King's son of Kush" in the 14th century BC. The accompanying hieroglyphs convey the Nubians' regard for the young pharaoh: "It is through love of you that we live."*

750 BC a Kushite king named Kashta ventured some 500 miles down the Nile from his capital city of Napata near the fourth cataract to Aswan, where he erected a stele that proclaimed him "King of Upper and Lower Egypt." Though he may have traveled as far north as Thebes, Kashta apparently made no attempt to exercise any royal powers and went home to Napata.

During the next generation the Napatans staked their claim. After ruling in Nubia for some 20 years, Kashta's son Piye took his army north. He may have arrived in response to a cry for help from the Theban priests, threatened by the impending invasion of Tefnakht, a warrior-prince from the delta 600 miles to the north, who was no friend to the theocracy at Thebes. Piye's Nubian army battled Tefnakht and his allies and conquered them all. The victorious Piye and his heirs became the pharaohs of the 25th Dynasty and ruled Egypt for the better part of a century.

Piye recorded his military triumphs in Egyptian hieroglyphs on a monumental victory stele in the Great Temple of Amen at Napata. Found among the ruins of the shrine in 1862, the gray granite slab now stands in Cairo's Egyptian Museum. Its text recounts the famous Nubian victory and offers revealing insights into the character of Piye himself. The inscription reports that Piye "raged like a panther" at the news of his enemy's advance and swore, "As Re loves me, as my father Amen favors me, I shall go north myself! I shall tear down his works. I shall make him abandon fighting forever!" Despite his apparent fury, Piye preferred negotiation to military confrontation, even—as the stele goes on to recount—sending his own queen

Rows of horses are led forth from the stables of the vanquished princes of Lower Egypt as tribute to Piye, the great Kushite king who conquered Egypt about 724 BC. The drawing replicates a fragmentary relief found on a wall of the Great Temple of Amen at Jebel Barkal, in Napata. Piye was so fond of horses he had them buried near his tomb standing up.

to parley with the wives of his enemy. He expressed no fondness for killing, even in wartime, and declared himself pleased to pardon any former foe who would swear him loyalty.

Piye gave no quarter, though, when it came to horses. He required conquered princes to give him the animals as tribute, and, of all the atrocities chargeable to his opponents, neglect of their horses was the one sin Piye considered unforgivable. As Piye's stele relates, while on a tour of the palace of King Nemrat of Hermopolis, which had fallen to Piye as spoils of war, "His Majesty proceeded to the stable of the horses and the quarters of the foals. When he saw they had been left to hunger he said to his submissive foe, 'I swear, as Re loves me, as my nose is refreshed by life: that my horses were made to hunger pains me more than any other crime you committed in your recklessness!' "

Piye's most illustrious dynastic successor proved to be his son Taharqa, who reigned from 690 to 664 BC, and, indeed, the Bible identified him as a threat to the Assyrians. After Taharqa's coronation, an inscription recorded the journey of his mother northward from Upper Nubia to Memphis, where "She rejoiced exceedingly after beholding the beauty of His Majesty crowned upon the throne of Upper and Lower Egypt."

In Egypt, Taharqa did not view himself as an outsider. During his reign he restored ancient Egyptian temples, erected new ones, and presided over a cultural revival in a realm that had declined sadly since the ancient days of glory. He also exhibited a fondness for sport. An inscription recounts a long-distance marathon race per-

DEATH AND BURIAL IN AN ALIEN LAND

Among the better-preserved mummies in Cairo's Egyptian Museum is one that poses a mystery all its own *(lower right)*. It is that of a man in his early twenties, who stood about five and a half feet tall. He was apparently of Nubian birth, as suggested by his appearance, his non-Egyptian name, Maiherperi, and his portrayal in the *Book of the Dead* that accompanied him to the grave. There he has been given dark skin rather than the red-brown color conventionally used by ancient artists to render Egyptians. Yet Maiherperi—whose name means Lion on the Battlefield—was buried in a well-appointed tomb in the Valley of the Kings, traditionally reserved for Egyptian royalty. Why and how did he come to be there?

Using his grave goods to date him, archaeologists place Maiherperi in the 15th century BC during Egypt's early New Kingdom. The high quality of these items and the care with which his body was mummified further indicate that Maiherperi must have been someone of importance to have received such treatment. Inscriptions on a box even call him "child of the nursery" and "fanbearer to the king."

Archaeologists theorize that Maiherperi was a Nubian prince brought to Egypt and raised at court. If he was indeed a royal personage, he would have been a pawn in Egypt's struggle to Egyptianize his people and gain cultural hegemony over them— which lends poignancy to his death so far from home.

The glass vase above, from Maiherperi's tomb, is attributable to the reign of Egypt's Amenhotep II (1450-1424 BC), but his so-called Osiris bed (below) could be of a later period. It consists of reed and linen stretched on a wooden frame, with the god's silhouette painted on it. Barley mixed with wet soil and spread on the image sprouted after the piece was placed in the tomb. The bed is almost identical to one found in the tomb of Amenhotep III's in-laws.

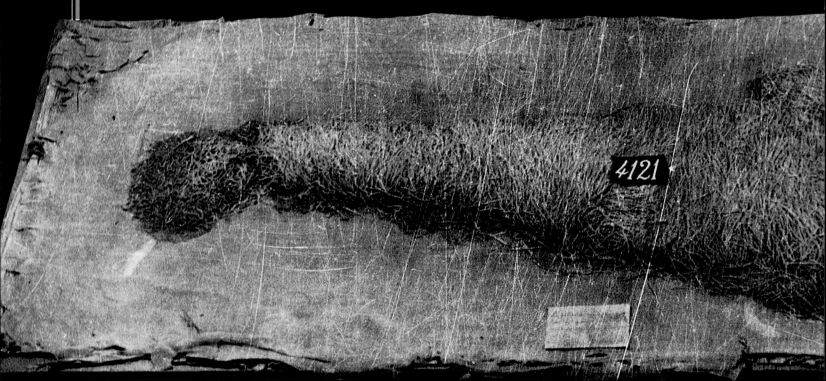

4121

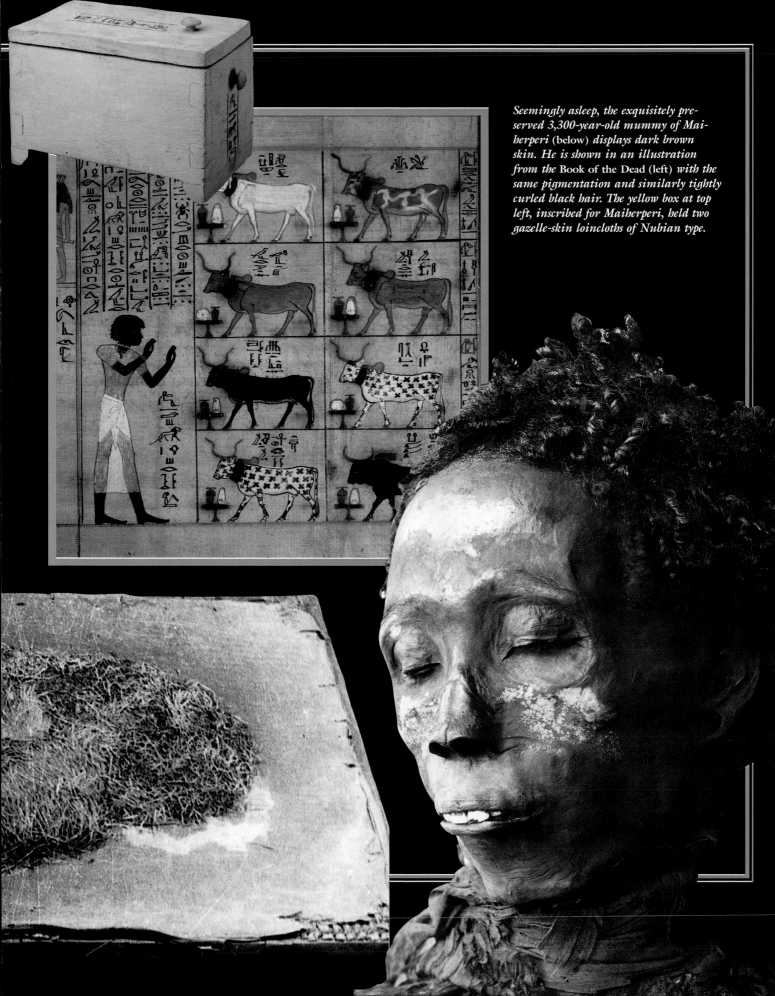

Seemingly asleep, the exquisitely preserved 3,300-year-old mummy of Maiherperi (below) displays dark brown skin. He is shown in an illustration from the Book of the Dead *(left) with the same pigmentation and similarly tightly curled black hair. The yellow box at top left, inscribed for Maiherperi, held two gazelle-skin loincloths of Nubian type.*

formed by the king's troops for his amusement. To avoid heat prostration, the competitors ran the 30-mile course through the desert at night. The king followed the runners on horseback and enjoyed himself so much he gave prizes to winners and losers alike.

In 667 BC Taharqa lost Egypt to the Assyrians, who had been cutting a swath throughout the Middle East. "I tore up the root of Kush," the Assyrian king Esarhaddon boasted in an inscription of his own, "and not one therein escaped to submit to me." Despite this humiliation, Taharqa survived the defeat of his armies and withdrew to Nubia, where he continued to reign as king until his death. Taharqa's nephew and successor, Tanwetamani, attempted to win back Egypt but failed and, like his uncle, retreated southward to end his days in Napata.

Much of what is known today about the lives of the Kushite kings of Egypt comes from the hieroglyphic inscriptions found in the ruins surrounding Jebel Barkal, a flat-topped butte looming over the Nubian plain where Napata lay, or from the royal cemeteries at El Kurru and Nuri, a few miles away. Here the pharaohs of the 25th Dynasty, their queens, and generations of later Nubian rulers lay entombed under small, steep-sided pyramids of stone. These structures puzzled archaeologists for many years, for they seemed to be solid and revealed no easy means of access.

In 1916 George A. Reisner was the head of an expedition in Nubia that was sponsored by Harvard University and the Boston Museum of Fine Arts. On the very day his team began excavating a pyramid near Jebel Barkal, Reisner discovered the means of entrance that later proved common to all such tombs. Some distance away from the pyramid, the builders had cut a gradually sloping stairway into the rock, which led to the burial chamber lying beneath the structure's base.

With the mystery of access solved, Reisner spent the next three years excavating the cemeteries of El Kurru, where all but the last of the Nubian pharaohs lay, and Nuri, where Reisner's team uncovered the impressive tomb of Taharqa himself. "We opened the stairway leading down to the burial chambers," Reisner recollected in 1918. "The men found in the debris filling the stairway a fragment of a stone figure on which was written the name of Taharqa." The once powerful ruler of Egypt and Kush lay under a ruined red-sandstone pyramid that may have stood 165 feet high and was certainly the largest ever constructed in the kingdom. Team members

Against the backdrop of the royal pyramids at Nuri in the Sudan, workers in this 1917 photo sort through some of the 1,070 mummiform figures called shawabtis that archaeologist George A. Reisner recovered from Taharqa's ruined tomb (visible as a low mound above the point of the left tent). The restored figures (right, below) fuse expressive, realistically rendered Nubian faces and rigid Egyptian form. Taharqa, 19 of his successors, and 53 of their queens were buried at Nuri.

also located the burial places of 19 later Nubian kings and 53 queens.

Although none of the tombs had escaped plundering, burials at both sites revealed enough to show that Nubians absorbed many funeral practices from their Egyptian neighbors. They attempted to mummify the royal corpses in the Egyptian manner and placed them in coffins decorated with gold, obsidian, and alabaster, accompanied by battalions of the small figurines called shawabtis that were thought to provide domestic services in the afterlife. According to Reisner, Taharqa's tomb alone contained more than a thousand of the beautifully carved stone shawabtis.

Yet Egyptian influence did not completely overshadow indigenous Nubian ways of burying the dead. Every burial chamber had at its center a masonry bench to support the traditional funerary bed where the mummy rested, a characteristically Nubian practice. And even in death, the Nubian kings continued to honor the steeds that had drawn their war chariots. Just 200 yards beyond the tombs of the kings at El Kurru, Reisner's team found a cemetery for horses. Inscriptions in the 24 graves identified their equine occupants as the property of Piye and three other 25th Dynasty kings. The horses, standing upright in their graves, wore shrouds of beaded net decorated with amulets of faience, cowrie shell, silver, and bronze. Silver collars found near some of the remains resembled those worn by stallions on a relief from the Great Temple of Amen at Napata, which depicted a cowering Egyptian prince offering tribute to his Kushite conqueror.

Napata, with its shrine of Amen, royal cemeteries, and the holy Jebel Barkal, retained its importance as a Kushite ritual center for some 400 years after the end of the 25th Dynasty. Around 300 BC the political and economic center of gravity in Nubia shifted southeastward from Napata to an area known as Meroë, located some 300 miles upriver between the fifth and sixth cataracts of the Nile. Some scholars speculate that this change occurred due to a power struggle between the Nubian kings and the influential priests of Amen, who chose every new monarch and held the crowns and scepters of those who had gone before. According to the Greek historian Diodorus Siculus, the clergy saw themselves as the god's earthly messengers. Amen, they claimed, communicated his divine will to their ears alone by means of a speaking statue. When they decided to exercise their influence on any affair of state, therefore,

In the flood-damaged tomb of Tanwetamani, successor to Taharqa and ruler of Kush from 664 to 657 BC, the twin goddesses Isis and Nephthys flank the passageway connecting the entrance room (foreground) to the arched burial chamber. Another protective deity, Hapi, leads the king to burial on the wall at left. The tomb was excavated in 1919 by Reisner at El Kurru, cemetery of most members of the Kushite 25th Dynasty of Egypt.

they were acting in the name of the deity. And, in thrall to their own superstitions, the kings obeyed, even going so far as to commit suicide. Diodorus Siculus tells how an early Meroitic king, Ergamenes, defied longstanding tradition and effected a clean sweep of the old regime by putting "the priests to the sword" instead and "thereafter ordered affairs after his own will."

Meroites continued to venerate Amen, and many temples to the Egyptian god were erected during this period. The structure dedicated to Amen at Meroë probably was intended to rival the Great Temple of Amen at the foot of Jebel Barkal. Nearly 500 feet long, Meroë's Amen Temple may have been the last built in the multi-roomed Egyptian style.

In contrast, temples honoring the Nubian lion god, Apedemak (page 45), who appears to have been only slightly less important than Amen, possessed only a single chamber, entered through an imposing pylon gate. The most well preserved of the lion temples still stand in the Meroitic religious and administrative centers of Naga and Musawwarat es-Sufra, 40 to 50 miles southwest of the capital.

Geography and economics also may have precipitated the southward move. As the setting for the political and economic nerve center of the kingdom, Meroë had many advantages over Napata, aside from its desirable distance from Amen's priesthood. Located in the fertile Butana Steppe east of the Nile, Meroitic cities prospered from both the raising of cattle and the cultivation of cereal crops. Musawwarat es-Sufra temple reliefs of large and apparently domesticated cattle suggest that the Meroites did not simply herd the animals but bred them as well. An enormous, enigmatic structure at Musawwarat es-Sufra called the Great Enclosure also may attest to the Meroites' skill with animals. A walled maze of enclosed rooms resembling pens and large plazas decorated with reliefs and three-dimensional sculptures of elephants led some scholars to propose that the huge beasts were kept and trained there. Though other scholars believe that the Great Enclosure served as a destination for caravans or for pilgrims attending religious festivals—with the pen-like spaces serving to protect the pack animals from lions—the many depictions of elephants undoubtedly reflect the beasts' local ceremonial and military significance.

The steppe's grasslands experienced reliable annual rainfall, which the farmers caught and collected in large reservoirs. Archaeologists investigating one of the basins in Musawwarat es-Sufra, more than 1,000 feet in diameter and 20 feet deep, estimated that its construction entailed the removal of 325,000 cubic yards of earth. The magnitude of such a project indicates that Meroë possessed a large and very efficiently managed labor force.

Meroë, rich in iron ore and timber, also generated considerable industrial activity. An English archaeological team from the University of Liverpool, headed by the archaeologist John Garstang, excavating the site between 1910 and 1914, found great heaps of iron slag, as well

The owner of this seventh-century BC alabaster jar, representing an antelope with bound legs, extracted ointment through the animal's open mouth. Like the Meroitic gold jackal shown at left, below, the vessel demonstrates the penchant of Nubian aristocrats for beautiful objects.

A giant dangles two elephants from a shoulder bar in this watercolor from the files of British archaeologist John Garstang, leader in 1910 of the first excavation of Meroë. It is thought to be a copy of a second- or third-century AD wall painting, now destroyed, that Garstang found in the royal quarter. Images of elephants, along with giraffes, crocodiles, lions, frogs, and other animals, are common in Meroitic art.

Lions representing aspects of the Meroitic deity Apedemak flank a ram, symbolic of the Meroitic state god Amen of Jebel Barkal, in this sandstone block from the Temple of Apedemak at Musawwarat es-Sufra. The panel and others like it were originally set into the walls above entrances to the temple, which lies about 50 miles south of Meroë.

as furnaces for smelting. A. H. Sayce, a member of the expedition, speculated that "Meroë must have been the Birmingham of ancient Africa." Though later investigators have disputed Sayce's suggestion that the city was the fountainhead of metallurgy for the northern part of the continent, Meroë was certainly an important iron center.

Meroë's most significant advantage, however, was its location at the point where great overland trade routes converged with the Nile, and the Nile itself became easily navigable far into the Sudan until it reached the Sudd, a swampy region in the south. Radiating out from Meroë, merchants and their beasts of burden—oxen, donkeys, horses, and by the first century BC, the resilient camel—traversed the tracks that led across desert and steppe, deep into the African heartland, to the Abyssinian highlands, to the Red Sea, or downstream into Egypt.

Political changes downriver had a direct effect on Nubian fortunes. When Egypt became the domain of the Ptolemies—Greek kings descended from one of the generals of the all-conquering Alexander the Great and heirs to this portion of his empire—it also became part of the Hellenistic world. The new Mediterranean trading partners gained in this political shift now looked to Egypt to supply them with the treasures of her own rich continent. And the Meroitic kingdom, conduit for the desired gold, salt, slaves, rare woods, ivory, and the skins of lions and leopards, reaped the rewards.

Around 200 BC its advanced and affluent society had developed a written script of its own. Meroitic texts of the age tantalize and frustrate modern scholars, however, for although the phonetic values of most of its 23 alphabetic symbols are understood along with certain proper names, the grammar and vocabulary of the Meroitic tongue remain, after more than 50 years of philological effort, untranslated.

In its own time, Meroë's fame spread far beyond Kush. Intrigued by tales of a great city far to the south of Egypt, Greek and Roman writers passed on descriptions, sometimes fantastically embroidered, from other sources. Herodotus, who in the fifth century BC traveled as far up the Nile as present-day Aswan, heard rumors that Meroë, some 60-days' march away, was a land of fabulous riches. Its inhabitants were giants, he was told, "the tallest and handsomest in the whole world," and possessed of such abundance that they buried their dead in crystal coffins and fettered their prisoners in chains of gold.

More reliable information about Meroë, however scanty, gradually began to emerge through the mists of hyperbole. Alexander the Great had opened a door by sending an expedition into Nubia in 332 BC, and by the following century, according to the chronicler Diodorus Siculus, the Meroitic monarch Ergamenes received a proper Greek education, including the study of philosophy. And Greek scholars were said to have found employment at Meroë's royal court. The Roman historian Pliny recorded the names of a number of Greeks known to have resided in the city of Meroë and garnered more information from reports of an expedition launched around AD 60 by the Roman emperor Nero. According to Pliny, elephants and rhinoceroses roamed just outside Meroë, while the city itself boasted fabulous temples to a deity he called Jupiter Hammon (Amen). The geographer Strabo described a palace with a garden of fruit trees. Humbler citizens, he said, lived in houses of brick or "interwoven pieces of split palm-wood."

Many centuries later, lured by the accounts of these classical writers, Europeans and Americans began to search for this fabled African city. In 1772 an eccentric Scottish explorer named James Bruce paid a visit to the Sudanese village of Bagrawiya, finding, he wrote, "heaps of broken pedestals and pieces of obelisks." His journal accurately declared that "it is impossible to avoid risking a guess that this is the ancient city of Meroë." Some 60 years after Bruce's visit, an amateur antiquarian named Giuseppe Ferlini rummaged and looted among the remains of Meroë's royal pyramids, blithely reporting that he had knocked the tops off several of these monuments in the process. Between 1842 and 1859 a German expedition headed by the famed Egyptologist C. R. Lepsius took a far more serious approach. The result of its investigations in Egypt and Nubia was a landmark book, *Monuments of Egypt and Ethiopia,* noted for the quality of its illustrations and text. And between 1905 and 1907 the American epigrapher and Egyptologist James H. Breasted incidentally recorded much of Nubia's written history in his quest to compile a survey of Egyptian inscriptions. But the arrival of Garstang's University of Liverpool Expedition in 1910 signaled the first attempt at scientific excavation of the site. Yet, even then, the expedition issued no definitive reports of results, and most of the original field notes and finds were widely and irretrievably scattered.

The most detailed knowledge of Meroë comes from George Reisner's Harvard-Boston expeditions and the 1965-71 work of the Canadian archaeologist Peter L. Shinnie for the University of Khartoum. The ruins of the city, made up of a square mile of earthen mounds, tumbled stone, and brick, and the slag heaps of ancient iron-working, lie on a terrace of silt and gravel on the east bank of the Nile. A stone, walled compound still holds the remains of the royal palace, government offices, small temples, and a royal bath. Outside this enclosure lay numerous temples and homes, built in a wide variety of styles, sizes, and patterns. Some of the mud-brick houses, presumably the residences of the better off, were solid and spacious, rising two or three stories in height, with vaulted rooms and yellow or whitewashed interior walls. Other, lowlier dwellings, with thinner walls and irregular floor plans, were clustered so closely together that archaeologists have been hard-pressed to differentiate between individual living units.

Two or three miles outside the city, on two ridges overlooking the desert, lie the pyramids of Meroitic kings and queens from the early third century BC to the fourth century AD. These monuments, together with inscriptions written in their own languages by Greek and Egyptian scribes in the temples of Lower Nubia, provided much of the information known about the rulers of the Kingdom of Meroë. These inscriptions gave archaeologists the names of many individual monarchs and some evidence relating to the reigns of specific rulers, such as King Natakamani and Queen Amanitore, who probably occupied the throne of Meroë during the lifetime of Jesus.

TREASURES OF A PLUNDERED PYRAMID

The steep-sided pyramids of Meroë, in the Sudan, were first seen by Europeans in the 1820s. As early as 1834 the structures excited one adventurer, an Italian by the name of Giuseppe Ferlini, to explore them for treasure. Believing that the tombs lay inside the pyramids (rather than below, in the rock), he recklessly leveled five of the monuments. Then, having turned up only saddles, metal bells, and a number of animal and human bones, he attacked the pyramid of Queen Amanishakheto, Meroë's ruler in the last decade of the first century BC. Inside it, Ferlini finally claimed his treasure: a cache of exquisite jewelry fashioned from gemstones and gold *(right)*.

A distance to the east, Ferlini later uncovered huge stone blocks that he suspected signaled even greater riches. Eager to keep the discovery a secret, he dismissed many of his workers. But instead of leaving, they took up lances and other weapons. Fearing for his life, Ferlini packed up Queen Amanishakheto's gold and escaped that night to a nearby settlement and then on to Europe, where he sold the pieces to museums in Berlin and Munich. The collection would not be reunited until 1992.

In another of Amanishakheto's shield rings, rearing cobras, or uraeuses, adorn the facade of a shrine, from which emerges the face of the god Amen, a ram's head crowned with a disk topped with a carnelian bead.

Two all-seeing wedjat eyes flank the head of the guardian god Sebiumeker on the gold ring below, one of eight so-called shield rings that Ferlini found inside Queen Amanishakheto's pyramid.

Concentric circles, rope braid, and heads of deities decorate the armlet below, the hinge of which is overlaid by a winged goddess. While on site, Ferlini took pains to keep the value of this and other pieces from his workers, whom he mistrusted. He carried the treasures from the pyramid concealed in leather pouches, then chased away the curious at gunpoint and buried the gold in the sand near his tent.

The royal couple devoted considerable energy to restoring old temples and building new ones. Their names appear in dedicatory inscriptions at the Great Temple of Amen in Meroë, in two shrines at Naga, and in the old cult center at Napata.

Queen Amanitore, as these inscriptions indicate, was no mere appendage to her husband but empowered in her own right, reigning jointly with him. Other queens, as indicated by their pyramids and by monuments bearing their names and images, ruled similarly. Each Nubian queen had the royal title candace, or kandake, which certain classical authors mistakenly believed to be a proper name instead of a regal appellation.

On reliefs decorating their tombs and temples, Amanitore and another first-century BC candace, Amanishakheto, spring to life as fierce and formidable Amazons. Single-handedly grasping their vanquished enemies by the hair, these massive warrior-queens raise well-fleshed arms to deliver the deathblow. They bear no resemblance to the sylphlike queens portrayed in the art of pharaonic Egypt or even of the old Nubian capital, Napata. The candaces' bodies bespeak the power and wealth that they possessed. The

Below, Greek-style columns and Roman-inspired arches dominate this kiosk, erected between the first and third centuries AD at Naga. The town's favorable location—on a caravan route leading to the Red Sea from the port of Wad Ban Naga, on the Nile—permitted its Nubian builders to sample an eclectic array of styles.

Above, Queen Amanitore, one of many powerful female rulers of Meroë, grasps her kingdom's enemies by the hair before striking them with a sword in this drawing copied from a pylon outside the Temple of Apedemak at Naga. Above the queen flies a vulture carrying a coiled rope, symbol of her control of the "circuit of the earth."

queens' faces bear ritual scars similar to those still worn by some present-day Africans.

Rallying to the battle cry of one of their candaces, an army from Meroë made its first active appearance in Roman history in 24 BC. When Rome took control of Egypt after Cleopatra's celebrated suicide put an end to Ptolemaic rule, the Nubian queen, thought to have been named Amanirenas, decided to test the strength of the Romans who took over. The newcomers occupied territories as far south as Aswan and had assumed control of the gold mines in the stretch of Lower Nubia known as the Dodekaschoenos, just south of Aswan. The Meroitic queen, who was, according to the Greek chronicler Strabo, "a very masculine sort of woman, and blind in one eye," sent her armies into the region on a campaign of plunder and pillage that culminated in the sacking of the Roman-held Holy Island at Philae and the destruction of statues of the then-reigning Roman emperor Augustus at Aswan.

Despite the candace's initial success, Strabo reported, she failed to daunt Rome. Gaius Petronius, the Roman prefect of Egypt, dispatched troops to Nubia on a punitive expedition. The soldiers trounced the Meroitic forces, drove the queen back upriver to her capital, and retaliated for the attacks at Philae and its environs by sacking Napata in turn. Meroë capitulated and an official agreement, known as the Treaty of Samos, established a border between Roman Egypt and the Meroitic kingdom. The Romans established a 400-man garrison at a site later known as Qasr Ibrim to guarantee the security of the new frontier.

Abandoning hostilities, the former enemies began instead to forge an enduring and mutually profitable commercial relationship. The evidence of this can be found in burials all over Nubia, where the graves of royal or merely wealthy figures from the first and second centuries AD yielded bronze work, ceramics, jewelry, silver, and glass from such distant outposts of the Roman Empire as Pergamon in Asia Minor. Their burial goods also revealed a lively mix of Mediterranean, Egyptian, and African styles and imagery. Giraffes, for instance, appeared alongside Greco-Roman vine leaves and Egyptian lotus.

Later Meroitic tombs, however, show signs of this once af-

RACE AGAINST TIME TO SAVE A BURIED CATHEDRAL'S MURALS

As the influence of ancient Egypt's religion faded in Nubia during the fifth and sixth centuries AD, Christianity became a strong force in peoples' lives. By the 16th century Islam gained the upper hand, and Christian monuments fell into ruin. When Polish archaeologist Kazimierz Michalowski started work in February 1961 at Faras, on the Nile's west bank just south of the Sudanese-Egyptian border, special conditions dictated that he work quickly. Faras, or Pakhoras, as it was known in ancient times, was the capital of one of three Christian kingdoms that suc-

ceeded the Ballana culture in the sixth century AD. The site had been partly investigated by British Egyptologist Frances Llewellyn Griffith before World War I, but it had lain undisturbed since. Now, as the water level rose behind the dam at Aswan, the excavation of Faras became urgent.

Michalowski started digging at the base of a 49-foot hill, on top of which stood the ruins of an Arab fort and a Coptic monastery. Two weeks later, he discovered the remains of a magnificent buried cathedral, built in AD 707, whose walls were covered with more than 120 well-

Saint Peter lays his hands on his name-sake Bishop Petros, patriarch of Faras from AD 974 to 999, in a detail of a mural from the cathedral. The size and location of the image challenged the restorers; painted some nine feet above floor level, the figures measure over seven feet tall.

Rocks and shrubs dot the land beyond a wall fragment exposed during Kazimierz Michalowski's excavation. The mural depicts the biblical story of Shadrach, Meshach, and Abednego. Hands raised in praise, they walk unharmed through the blazing furnace, sheltered by the wings of the archangel Michael.

preserved murals. The great value of the paintings—and the imminent flood—forced him to make a painful decision. "We had to give up a more thorough investigation of other elements," he wrote, "and concentrate our efforts on saving the paintings."

Expert restorers from the National Museum in Warsaw were summoned to cut the murals from the walls. Then the artworks were wrapped in cotton blankets and packed in crates for shipment to museums in Khartoum and Warsaw. The rescue occurred not a moment too soon. "Hardly had the expedition finished nailing up the cases for removal," Michalowski reported, "when the Nile water reached the level of the hill on which the excavation had taken place. Some months later, the tops of a few palm trees emerging from the lake were all that remained to mark the spot where Faras had once stood."

Symbols of the four evangelists ring an image of Christ at the center of a crucifix in the painting at right. The legends near the head of each of the apostles, and above the cross, are in Coptic, the liturgical language of Nubia's Christian Coptic Church.

fluent kingdom's slow decline. Excavations of sites from the third and fourth centuries AD reveal that Nubia's rulers no longer had the means to erect great shrines and monuments on a scale commensurate with those of their predecessors. Even the royal pyramids were smaller and less solidly built. But nothing spoke so clearly of the end of Meroë's golden age as the virtual disappearance of imported luxury items from the goods that furnished the burial chambers.

Changes far beyond Nubia helped hasten Meroë's decline. After AD 200 the Romans began to take advantage of other trade routes, abandoning the arduous desert trails controlled by Meroë, shipping goods instead across the Red Sea and overland through Arabia to speed commerce with the lucrative markets farther east. Rome also managed to impoverish Egypt by carrying off the lion's share of her agricultural production to fill the granaries of the empire. Instead of a crossroads, Meroë now lapsed into a backwater and an endangered one at that. Nomads from the desert, once an occasional problem, became an outright threat. By the fourth century AD, the Noba people had emerged from the wilderness to the west of the Nile and taken control of the once-wealthy towns and cities of the Butana Steppe, probably overrunning Meroë itself.

The invasion of the Noba marked the end of the Meroitic period, its literacy, monumental architecture, and political and religious traditions. Meroë's heartland, the Butana region, plunged into a dark age lasting from AD 350 to 550. So completely did the Meroites seem to disappear that in 1907 when Reisner discovered graves from this period just a few miles south of Aswan in Lower Nubia, he realized the people to whom they belonged had emerged long after the C-group and thus could not have sprung directly from them. To give them a place in the chronology, he assigned them the letter *X* and referred to them as the X-group.

The excavation of a number of large mounds at the twin cities of Ballana and Qustul, across the Nile from one another just north of the second cataract, revealed that the X-group, now called the Ballana culture for its largest necropolis, was but the next generation in the long-lived Nubian family tree. The perceptive Amelia Edwards noticed the mounds, thought by the local inhabitants to be natural formations, on her trip up the Nile in 1874. "We came upon a new wonder," Edwards wrote, "namely, upon two groups of scattered tumuli, one on the eastern, one on the western bank. Not volcanic

The skeleton of a fourth-century AD king lies in Tomb 80, which Walter B. Emery opened in 1932, at Ballana, a necropolis on the Nile about 20 miles north of Sudan. The ruler was laid on a wooden bed with jewelry, weapons, bronze and silver vessels, several animals, and eight servants. A foot-tall silver headpiece embossed with glass and semiprecious stones (right) *crowned his head. The cobras and the ram reveal that Lower Nubia kings still owed allegiance to Egyptian and Meroitic gods.*

forms these; not even accidental forms, if one may venture to form an opinion from so far off."

Although Edwards guessed correctly about the origin of the mounds, more than 50 years passed before Walter B. Emery, British archaeologist for the Egyptian Antiquities Service, climbed to the top of one and came to the same conclusion. Emery began excavations in 1931 and, during the following three seasons, explored 180 tombs at the two sites. About 40 of the tombs contained enormous riches, including jewelry, silver vessels, inlaid chests of wood and ivory, weapons, lamps and incense burners, glass, textiles, and pottery. The most telling of the burial goods were 10 crowns of hammered silver, covered with semiprecious stones and adorned with royal symbols and representations of Horus, Isis, and Amen. Three of the most ornate crowns bear a silver relief of a ram's head topped by a crest of stylized silver plumes. Representations of kings and queens carved on the temples of Meroë and Naga wear the same emblem.

While Emery believed that "the X-group tumulus is the direct descendant of the Meroitic pyramid, with the entrance stairway concealed under the superstructure," the burials strongly resembled those of an even earlier antecedent, the Kerma burials of Upper Nubia. Approximately 2,000 years before, the Kerma buried their dead under similar tumuluses, on funeral beds, and with human sacrifices. Clearing one of the tombs, Emery's team came upon a scene reminiscent of Reisner's find at Kerma some 20 years earlier: "Apparently the death of one of these ancient monarchs entailed the sacrifice of all those nearest to him: his wife, his slaves, male and female, guards, grooms, horses, and even his dogs. We found many of the human bodies lying face downwards as if they had been struck with axe-blows from behind, and others who had probably met their death by strangulation. As we cleared their poor mouldering bones we could visualize that scene of horror as the body of the King was laid in his tomb, followed by terror-stricken men and women, dragged down into the darkness by their slayers."

As if to confirm this unbroken thread of civilization, excavators uncovered, at Qasr Ibrim, some 100 miles south of Aswan, information on the lives and beliefs of Nubians for a period that extended from an era before the 25th Dynasty and continued through

Nubia's Meroitic, Ballana, and Christian periods. Here, where the worlds of Rome and Meroë once converged, the dry desert air preserved even such fragile materials as woven baskets. An archaeologist described some of the baskets, fashioned from palm leaves and dating from the third and fourth centuries AD, as being in "such good condition that they could be used for shopping right away."

Excavations at Qasr Ibrim, begun in 1961, posed a considerable logistical challenge. The site proved too rich in remains to allow the work to be completed before the rising waters of the Aswan High Dam flooded the surrounding area. Fortunately, because of the elevated position of the old fortress, most of the ruin today stands clear of the maximum high-water line. Expeditions can work from houseboats and tugs, with all supplies, equipment, and team members ferried in at the beginning of each four-month-long excavation season. Virtually cut off from the outside world, the archaeologists conduct their investigations of three millennia of Nubian history on an island quite literally afloat in time.

As an important administrative center, where brigades of scribes once bent over papyrus and parchment, Qasr Ibrim housed documents in many languages, including bilingual texts that may, in time, yield vital clues to the elusive meanings of the Meroitic script. And as the site of several great temples probably dedicated to the worship of Isis, it held the last surviving remnants of the old pagan faith of Egypt and Nubia, which endured here until well into the sixth century AD. Until then, pilgrims visited Qasr Ibrim, carving the outlines of their footprints in the shrines, but residents, presaging the conversion to Christianity that eventually swept across all of Nubia, hedged their bets for salvation by inscribing crosses in their tombs.

MYSTERY OF THE SACRED MOUNT

Beside the Nile, some 200 miles north of the city of Khartoum, a lone sandstone butte soars 320 feet, with a strangely shaped pinnacle rearing to one side. Today this landmark is known in Arabic as Jebel (Mount) Barkal, though in the 15th century BC, the Egyptian conquerors of Nubia referred to it as The Pure Mountain. Here the new rulers founded Napata, a city that for four centuries marked the southern limit of Egypt's African empire. Later, after the Egyptians had withdrawn from Nubia, Napata became the northern capital and chief cult center of an independent Nubian kingdom called Kush. In the eighth century BC, the kings of Kush conquered Egypt and ruled as its 25th Dynasty.

Today, beneath the butte's shadow, Napata's ruins may still be seen. During the early 20th century, these were the focus of intensive investigation by famed archaeologist George A. Reisner of Boston's Museum of Fine Arts. In the 1980s another museum-sponsored expedition, under the leadership of Timothy Kendall, resurveyed and mapped the site, paying particular attention to the pinnacle.

Some observers back in the 1820s had become convinced that Jebel Barkal's pinnacle was a much weathered colossal statue wearing the tall, knobbed crown of Upper Egypt. Much later, in 1941, visitors to the site scanned the outcrop through binoculars and spied an inscription near the top bearing the names of two royal figures. Determined to investigate, Timothy Kendall and a rock climber scaled the 284-foot spire *(above)* in 1987. Although it proved to be a natural formation after all, it contained at its summit remains of a remarkable monument of the Kushite pharaoh Taharqa (690-664 BC). Probing further, Kendall's team discovered that the ancients had seen something wonderful in the pinnacle's odd shape—and that what they saw had had an enormous impact on the course of Egyptian and Nubian history.

During the 1989 excavating season, Tim Kendall's team made a complete survey of the Jebel Barkal temples and pyramids, the first one to be conducted since the 1840s, when the site was explored by a Prussian expedition. One of the team's objectives was to create a highly accurate, up-to-date map, which incorporated the plans of all buildings that had been excavated since 1916 by Reisner, by an Italian team from the University of Rome, and by Kendall's own team.

Taking all of the information that they had collected, Kendall's group then accomplished the second of their goals. They fed the data into a computer and obtained an interactive, three-dimensional computer model allowing them to see how the Jebel Barkal structures appeared more than 2,500 years ago.

As the bulbous-topped pinnacle stands silhouetted in twilight, project surveyor David A. Goodman prepares to fix the site's position in relation to the polestar. To establish true north, Goodman uses a computerized distance measure and a theodolite.

Goodman takes further measurements from the edge of the Jebel Barkal cliff, recording the cliff's height with respect to the sanctuary at its base and the circumference of the butte's flat surface. In the distance can be seen small pyramids from the third and first centuries BC, marking royal Kushite tombs.

Shot late in the day, a low-angled aeri-al photograph (above) starkly highlights the architectural ruins of the temple complex. Measurements of the site and of individual temples were used to cre-ate the computer-generated rendering (right) of the buildings in their prime.

Jebel Barkal, held by Kushites to be the dwelling place of Amen, god of the sun, creation, and kingship, became the site of all their coronations. The people of Kush, like their counterparts in Egypt, believed their king to be the blessed son of Amen but selected him in a manner that was peculiarly their own. The eligible males were brought to the temple at the foot of the butte and paraded before the god's effigy, which was thought to have oracular powers. Somehow it signaled its choice, and the selected one thus had the crown of Kush bestowed upon him. But there was risk attached: The Greek historian Diodorus Siculus commented that the statue could also order the death of the king, who was expected to commit suicide upon receipt of the command.

At top, Tim Kendall records fragmentary reliefs in the Great Temple of Amen. Above, he and conservator Susanne Gänsicke expose an unusual ram-headed column capital in the palace debris. Though much damaged by centuries of sandstorms, Nile floods, and human intrusions, Jebel Barkal's temples still yield important data on Kushite history and religious beliefs.

Aerial photos of the Jebel Barkal sanctuary, such as the one at far right, helped Kendall's team determine positions of unexcavated buildings in relation to excavated ones. Their site plan (inset) locates the pinnacle (A) and shows how the temples cluster around it in an arc. On the right are the two great parallel shrines to Amen; on the left lie temples to the great goddesses (B); and in front stand the palace (C) and a yet unexcavated temple (D) pointed toward the pinnacle with the inscription bearing royal names at its top.

Not only was the inscription near the pinnacle's top too high to be seen with the naked eye, it was also separated from the butte by a deep gorge. How and why the Nubians had put hieroglyphs there remained a puzzle. When Kendall and project manager Cynthia Shartzer tried to examine the writing with a telescope in 1986, they could barely make out the much-eroded message. However, they could see, on the cliff edge opposite the pinnacle, deep holes that still retained mortar impressions of the logs that had been set into them.

To learn more, Kendall took climbing lessons from mountaineer Paul Duval, and the two tackled the pinnacle in 1987. Rappelling off the cliff into the gorge, then scaling the shaft's backside, they reached the top, where they could read the names of two kings *(below)*. They also found remnants of a once-gilded monument of Taharqa, the last great Kushite pharaoh of Egypt, as well as direct evidence of the Kushites' amazing engineering skills *(drawing, far right)*.

Secured with rope, Kendall rappels down the face of the pinnacle. Above him looms Taharqa's inscribed panel, which once measured 10 feet by 5 feet. Before him is a man-made alcove that contains an empty socket for a small statue, now lost. The cavity displays traces of the stone-and-mortar sidewalls that had sheltered the piece from the relentless winds.

Though only the middle third of the inscription survives, it is enough to reveal that the carving had been commissioned by Taharqa in the seventh century BC for the purpose of proclaiming his victories over enemies east and west. Three centuries later it was restored by King Nastasen, whose name appears above. Regularly spaced holes in the stone still contain bronze nails, a clear sign that the panel had once been covered with a reflective gold sheet.

Re-creating the effect of the gold sheet that had gleamed atop the pinnacle, Kendall covers the carved panel with a sheet of Mylar. The discovery of a series of regular holes cut into the shaft and the opposing cliff indicated the position of log platforms, scaffolds, and lifting devices (below). These had enabled the Kushites to raise themselves, stone, mortar, gold, and a statue to the otherwise inaccessible summit.

While it was clear that the temples at Jebel Barkal's base had been oriented with the pinnacle in mind, no one knew why. Then team member Lynn Holden observed that ancient frontal views of the butte had included a rearing cobra, crowned with either a sun disk or the tall, knobbed crown of Upper Egypt. This seemed to suggest that the Egyptians and the Kushites had visualized a snake in the rock's curious shape. The team confirmed Holden's theory by observing that the rock did resemble a cobra and that, depending on the angle, the cobra could be construed as wearing one or the other of the two crowns. For both Kushites and Egyptians, the primary symbol of kingship was a rearing cobra called a uraeus, which the king wore on his crown. They believed this symbol, like kingship itself, was granted by the god Amen. It seems likely, therefore, that they recognized the butte as Amen's home and the pinnacle as a great royal head or crown and a source of royal power in the Nile Valley. Thus Napata emerged as a sacred city of temples and later as a center of all royal ceremonies.

Napata's temple complex rises again (left) *in a computer model accurately superimposed on a photo. Here, viewed from the east, the pinnacle resembles a uraeus topped by Upper Egypt's knobbed crown. A temple relief of Taharqa offering to Amen and his wife* (above) *shows the pinnacle from the west, seen as a cobra crowned with a sun disk.*

WEST AFRICA: KINGDOMS OF SAVANNA AND FOREST

The verdant flood plain of the Niger River flashed into view in the distance, a stark contrast to the sunbaked savanna all around. To Susan and Rod McIntosh, American graduate students in archaeology, the green vista was a welcome sight. For several weeks during the winter of 1975, the two of them had been nursing their secondhand Peugeot 404 over rutted roads through the parched landscape of Senegal and western Mali in search of tells—earthen mounds built up over centuries of human settlement. Ahead, finally, the McIntoshes caught a glimpse of civilization—the centuries-old city of Jenné, with its magnificent mosque dominating the skyline.

Jenné lies in the Republic of Mali, near the confluence of the Niger River—Africa's third longest—and its tributary the Bani. Their combined flow creates a curious geologic feature almost unknown among the world's waterways—an inland delta. Just north of Jenné, the riverbed divides into a myriad of twisting channels, which snake through the level terrain for 200 miles, all the way to Timbuktu, where the meandering segments reunite for the remainder of the Niger's course to the Atlantic.

Since time immemorial, the rainy season has produced the months-long flooding that inundates this region, spawning a wealth of cereal crops and driving schools of fish into the ephemeral streams

Symbol of royal power in the West African city-state of Benin, this snarling brass leopard served as a ceremonial water vessel for the king. Filled through an opening in the head, it dispensed its contents through the nostrils.

crisscrossing the delta. Jenné had long benefited from its propitious setting; the city's bounty was legendary. "This place," wrote the 16th-century Moorish chronicler Leo Africanus, "exceedingly aboundeth with barlie, rice, cattell, fishes, and cotton."

Scanning the lush panorama, the McIntoshes noted the proliferation of abandoned tells, easily discernible in the flat delta landscape, and conjectured that the region must have supported a sizable populace long before medieval Jenné had been founded. With a stir of excitement, they headed for the town to get a night's rest before taking a closer look at the tells. Shortly after the McIntoshes' arrival in Jenné, however, Rod was struck with bacillary dysentery, and the couple was forced to depart. Only months later, while examining some aerial photographs, did they detect the outlines of a vast tell. What they were soon to discover at the tell would establish the reputations of the young graduate students as prominent authorities in the field of African archaeology. Even two decades later, this remarkable site would still occupy much of their efforts.

The tell lay some two miles from Jenné, on an abandoned channel of the Bani River. Nearly as large as the modern town, the teardrop-shaped mound was surrounded by a flurry of smaller tells—by the McIntoshes' count at least 65 within a two-and-a-half-mile radius. In January 1977 the couple finally surveyed the site in person. Walking across the man-made hillock for the first time, they marveled at the treasure trove beneath their feet: Glass beads, potsherds, pieces of stone bracelets, and bits of corroded metal littered the dark soil. Under the scattered artifacts, mud-brick foundations and the truncated remains of a fortresslike wall still showed plainly. Clearly, sometime in the long-forgotten past, the mound had been the center of a flourishing community, but when and for how long?

After recruiting local helpers, the McIntoshes set to work. Their aim, in the few short months before the rains set in, was to develop a chronological framework for interpreting the history of the town, dubbed Jenné-jeno—ancient Jenné. They began by digging four sample pits, two near the center of the mound and two on its periphery. The rewards were immediate: The artifacts—ceramics, copper ornaments, iron knives, and clay toys among them—numbered in the hundreds of thousands.

The McIntoshes and their crew burrowed down some 20 feet before encountering sterile soil. This alone suggested Jenné-jeno's great antiquity, but it was not until they received the radiocarbon dat-

ing for charcoal and stored grain extracted from the pit's lowest level that the town's profound age came to light. The charcoal had come from a cooking fire lit in 250 BC. By cross-referencing this and other dated samples with associated soil layers and pottery styles, the couple determined that Jenné-jeno had been inhabited from the third century BC through the 14th century AD. At that point—following more than 1,600 years of continuous occupation—the city was mysteriously abandoned.

Taken by themselves, these findings were extraordinary. When viewed in the context of accepted historical convention, however, they were revolutionary. Most scholars had long assumed that urban centers such as Jenné-jeno did not develop in West Africa until the 13th century AD or later and that they had resulted from outside impetus. Around then, the reasoning went, North African Arabs blazed trade routes south through the Sahara, stimulating the growth of market towns in the savanna and forest lands beyond. But here, buried under the silt of the Niger's Inland Delta, was indisputable proof that a complex indigenous society had sprung forth on its own and flourished for nearly a millennium before Arab contact.

Puzzling out the riddle of Jenné-jeno's long history and precipitous decline was left to another season of excavation, undertaken four years after the first. In the meantime, the McIntoshes had published their initial findings, completed their degrees, and joined the anthropology faculty of Rice University in Houston, Texas. They returned to Jenné on New Year's Day, 1981, to resume their careful probing of the mound. What the two of them discovered over the ensuing months shattered even more scholarly presumptions about the course of civilization building in West Africa.

Jenné-jeno's earliest residents lived in round pole and mat reed structures plastered over with mud. Faint impressions of the woven mats could still be seen on fragments of wall plaster baked

An aerial view of part of the Niger's Inland Delta shows the modern town of Jenné on the Bani River (left) *and, less than two miles to its south, the ancient settlement of Jenné-jeno* (upper right). *Already a wealthy mercantile center when Muslim traders arrived in the eighth century, Jenné-jeno may have been abandoned for the new Islamic Jenné because of the old city's associations with paganism.*

Jenné-jeno

and hardened by the heat of accidental fires. Bones and carbonized grain unearthed in cooking pits attested to regular consumption of perch and catfish, supplemented by waterfowl, tortoise, crocodile, and rice, sorghum, and millet. Over the next two centuries, the residents added domesticated beef to their diet.

Most surprising was the discovery that these capable agriculturalists had been skilled ironsmiths as well. As early as the third century BC, Jenné-jeno's residents were smelting iron on an unprecedented scale, as evidenced by relics of furnaces and quantities of iron slag. In order to get the ore needed to forge iron, the town probably traded surplus food with the ore-rich region of Benedougou, 50 miles to the southeast.

Between the fourth and the 10th century AD, Jenné-jeno blossomed into a true entrêpot, with a network of satellite villages—the smaller tells the McIntoshes had noticed—encircling the city. Poised at the confluence of the Niger's riverine trade, the city became the hub of a far-flung trade network. The waterways teemed with long, narrow canoes called pirogues, their holds stacked with Jenné-jeno's abundance: baskets of blackened catfish (smoked to preserve them), flasks of fish oil, and mounds of onions and red African rice.

With its plentiful produce, the city bought slabs of Saharan salt and raw materials. Iron was not the only metal employed by Jenné-jeno's homegrown industries. Copper hair ornaments unearthed in the ruins of homes dating from the period testify to the city's traffic with mines as far as 600 miles to the north. And from the gold fields of the savanna and the forest far to the south and west must have come the raw material to fashion an earring disinterred from beneath the ancient city wall. Reminiscent of a bird in flight, the delicate ornament was probably the work of a local smith.

At the city's zenith, from AD 800 to 1000, Jenné-jeno and its subordinate communities boasted a population of some 50,000 and covered 100 acres. Villas surrounded by privacy walls created a labyrinth of shaded alleyways barely wide enough for two persons to

Looted from sites along the Middle Niger in contravention of Malian law, these two terra cottas are orphans in time. While the figures at left, below, may represent actual people—a rich couple, given the jewelry worn on their necks, wrists, and ankles—the three-headed, three-breasted statuette above may have had protective or ancestral significance. Given the illegal and unscientific manner of the pieces' removal, no one will ever know.

pass. By this time, Jenné-jeno was peopled by a complex hierarchy of specialists, including potters, metalsmiths, weavers, leatherworkers, and poet-historians known as griots.

Oral traditions still repeated today indicate that blacksmiths, whose ironworking art was steeped in mystery, enjoyed the status of priest-leaders. To the farmers of the West African savanna, iron was far more precious than gold, for one cannot fashion a hoe from gold. It is no surprise, then, that they venerated—and feared—those few who knew the mystical secret of turning raw ore into durable metal implements and also no surprise that the secret was well guarded by the blacksmiths' clique.

As a result of their seemingly supernatural powers, blacksmiths assumed a variety of roles, not just in Jenné-jeno but in many West African societies. Among the Bambara people of West Africa, the village smith, called the *doni-kèla*—someone who knows—was charged with divining the future. Blacksmiths also arbitrated village disputes, acted as political advisers to kings, and performed the important ritual of circumcision. Their skills as doctors were sometimes astounding. Scholars have determined that West African blacksmiths successfully inoculated patients against smallpox—using the tip of a red-hot poker and a live virus—long before the procedure was developed in Europe.

The blacksmiths' spiritual preeminence started to wane around the beginning of the second millennium AD, as Islam began making inroads among the population. The first to convert were merchants, perhaps hoping to smooth business relations with their North African contacts. Eventually, the entire society embraced the Muslim faith wholeheartedly. By the 14th century a new Islamic Jenné, then as now dominated by an impressive mosque, had arisen a few miles to the northwest of the old city. Jenné-jeno and its dependent villages lay abandoned, the ground upon which they stood "defiled" by the "pagan" rituals of the past, and the once-thriving metropolis slowly disappeared from view and memory beneath river-borne silt.

As the McIntoshes' excavations at Jenné-jeno dramatically illustrated, West Africa's

Excavated by the McIntosh expedition to Jenné-jeno in 1981, this headless, reclining figure was probably a family or cult object and is one of the few Middle Niger terra cottas found in its original stratigraphic context. Dated to the period of Jenné-jeno's decline, the statuette had been buried in a rubbish heap on the edge of the dying town, its head severed from the body. The act may have symbolized the people's break with their pagan past.

history is far older and more extensive than previously believed by Westerners. Long before the incursion of Arab merchants, local trade networks had developed, based on the exchange of resources among the region's diverse ecological zones. These zones, stretching in east-west belts from the Sahara Desert southward to the rain forest along the Gulf of Guinea, have to a large degree determined the pattern and the history of the cultures within them.

To the north lie the thirsty stretches of the Sahel, a zone whose name comes from the Arabic word *sahil,* or shore. The term is certainly appropriate, for, like a shoreline, the Sahel borders the great ocean of the Sahara Desert from Mauritania to Chad. With few exceptions, the sere expanse is relieved only by short grasses and the occasional acacia tree. Farming in the Sahel is a marginal proposition at best. The early towns of the Sahel, much like seaports, were ideally situated to provision the caravans making the trans-Saharan voyage—and to take a cut of the goods passing through.

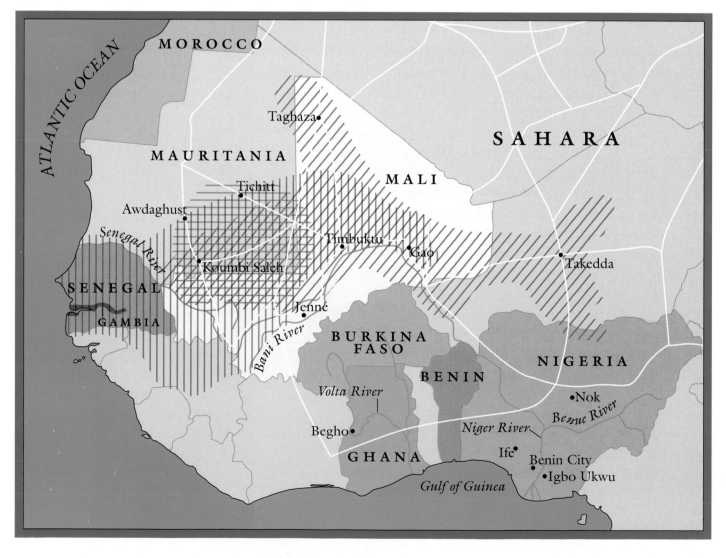

Southward from the Sahel extend the plains of West Africa's savanna. Seared by six months of heat and flooded by six months of rain, the region supports waving tracts of sorghum and millet interspersed, with stands of thorny brush and baobab trees. Antelope, wild buffalo, ostrich, and small game—an important source of meat, hides, and feathers for early inhabitants—once populated its vast, open stretches. Long ago, alluvial gold was panned from the rivers of the savanna.

Still farther south, where rainfall becomes more regular, savanna gives way to mixed woodlands. Thickets of oil palms thrive and yams grow in profusion. Kola trees produce a bounty of kola nuts—a mild stimulant similar in effect to caffeine—much prized by the ancient and modern peoples of West Africa.

Finally, near the well-watered Gulf of Guinea coast, the woods give way to sweltering rain forest. Towering ebony, mahogany, and ironwood trees form a dense canopy, shading mangrove swamps and inland lagoons. The region's gold-bearing granite rocks provided forest dwellers with an important source of wealth.

Together, these ecological zones compose an area as large as the United States. Disparate as they are in climate and vegetation, they share a common attribute that has had an immense impact on human habitation from the earliest times to the present: West Africa lies entirely within the tropics and a multitude of debilitating and deadly diseases are endemic to the region. Here no river or body of fresh water is free of intestinal parasites or the snails that transmit schistosomiasis (liver flukes) to humans and cattle. Malaria, dysentery, leprosy, and sleeping sickness—brought on by the tsetse fly—are all prevalent. In addition, other scourges, such as locusts, sometimes attack crops in sky-darkening waves, and termites, living in mounds up to 15 feet high, can make short work of wooden structures. Poisonous snakes and insects, too, abound. In the face of such an inhospitable environment, the achievements of West Africans over the centuries appear all the more remarkable.

At a site called Dhar Tichitt in Mauritania, American and French archaeologists have laid bare the remains of an extensive hunting and farming community that existed from 1500 to 500 BC. The site now lies in the Sahara, but during the moister climate of the period the archaeologists studied, the upper limits of the Sahel extended farther north, permitting a settled agricultural lifestyle. Dhar Tichitt's inhabitants herded cattle and goats and subsisted on a mix

A map of West Africa delineates modern-day boundaries and some of the historical cultures that occupied the land. Dominating the central savanna were the great empires of Ghana, Mali, and Songhay, which flourished with the expansion of trade with the Arab north. Camel-borne merchants crossed the Sahara on ancient caravan trade routes (white lines), then transferred their goods to mules and human porters for the journey to Begho, Ife, and other towns near the Gulf of Guinea. Some of these southern settlements, such as Benin City, also maintained commerce with European traders along the coast.

of wild grain and cultivated millet. Around 1000 BC they began building masonry compounds protected by high walls and fortified gates—an indication of guarded affluence.

Well to the south of Dhar Tichitt in the light woodlands fringing the Black Volta River in present-day Ghana, excavators have discovered another farming culture they call Kintampo. By 1400 BC Kintampo farmers were cultivating oil palms, cowpeas, and yams in forest clearings beside their wattle-and-daub dwellings. But agriculture was not the Kintampo people's only stock in trade. From a nearby dolomite mine came stone to fashion finely wrought tools, bracelets, and arrowheads. The large quantity of artifacts so far uncovered suggests that these items were being produced not only for use within the community but also for trade.

But the most striking archaeological evidence of early West African trade comes from the burial mounds, or tumuluses, dotting the plains of Senegal and Mali. The tombs, ranging in date from the middle of the first millennium AD to 900 or later, contain regally appointed corpses and hoards of gold, copper, and iron—along with sacrificial victims. According to archaeologists, the wealth and ceremony attending these burials indicate the emergence of powerful chiefdoms and local states grown rich on the control of resources and interregional trade. Scholars speculate that by the

Arranged in a circle, these ancient standing stones in the Gambia enclose a burial mound, or tumulus, that dates from pre-Islamic times. The sandstone megaliths—which can protrude up to 10 feet above the ground—are often built on top of a subterranean retaining wall that symbolically confines the spirit of the dead. Thousands of these stone enclosures dot the landscapes of West Africa.

sixth or seventh centuries AD, increasingly complex sites were emerging all over West Africa.

In the savanna, the consolidation of these states gave rise to vast trading empires: Ghana, Mali, Songhay. These empires were despotic and progressively eliminated older, local-based authority, but their dazzling glory is remembered to this day in the songs and folk tales of West Africa. Ruled by divine kings who presided over glittering courts, the empires of the savanna astounded the most urbane of the Arab and European travelers who visited them. The standard of living they afforded their subjects—in terms of goods and security—was on a par with any of the world's medieval states. By AD 1500 gold, ivory, and slaves exported through the empires' trade channels had become critical commodities influencing the economies of both Arab North Africa and western Europe.

The vast mercantile empires of the savanna never held sway in the woodlands and forests to the south; there, power was concentrated in kingdoms and city-states. Theirs was a great spiritual legacy—one that produced a sublime art. The last of these mighty forest states, the Kingdom of Benin, monopolized the flourishing Atlantic-European trade begun in the 15th century. It would prove the kingdom's greatest boon and its ultimate ruin.

The Arab geographer al-Fazari, writing in the court records of the caliph of Baghdad in AD 773, refers to Ghana as the "Land of Gold." The earliest of West Africa's savanna empires, Ghana extended west from the Niger Bend to the Senegal River. (It should be noted that ancient Ghana encompassed parts of modern Mauritania, Senegal, and Mali and lay entirely outside the borders of the present-day Republic of Ghana.) Based on al-Fazari's citation, which suggests an established empire, scholars posit a fifth- or sixth-century AD origin for Ghana.

The market towns of the savanna had, by that time, established themselves in an enviable commercial position. Sandwiched between the northern "ports" of the Sahel and the gold-rich cities of the southern forest, they exercised the controlling role of middleman. Probably in a bid to win protection for their share of the region's long-distance trade, the savanna city-states were forced together into a kind of confederation that took its name from the most powerful leader—the *ghana,* or king.

Wings outstretched, this 11th-century bronze ibis was unearthed in the early 1900s from a tumulus in the Gao region of Mali. Since the artifact was hastily removed from the site, it is not known whether it was in fact part of the original burial rites. Ancient West Africans revered ibises for the birds' supposed oracular powers.

Some idea of the pomp and majesty attending Ghana's royal court can be gleaned from the 11th-century *Book of Roads and Kingdoms,* a travelogue composed by the Moorish geographer al-Bakri of Córdoba. "The king," writes al-Bakri, "adorns himself like a woman, wearing necklaces round his neck and bracelets on his forearms, and when he sits before the people he puts on a high cap decorated with gold and wrapped in a turban of fine cloth."

The geographer then goes on to describe the proceedings of the empire's civil court: "When the king gives audience to his people, to listen to their complaints and to set them to rights, he sits in a pavilion around which stand 10 horses with gold embroidered trappings. Behind the king stand 10 pages holding shields and gold-mounted swords; on his right are the sons of princes of his empire, splendidly clad and with gold plaited in their hair. The door of the pavilion is guarded by dogs of an excellent breed who almost never leave the king's presence, and who wear collars of gold and silver." Permission to approach the king, says al-Bakri, is signaled by the beating of a log drum called a *daba;* in presenting themselves, the king's subjects "fall on their knees and sprinkle dust on their heads, for this is their way of showing respect for him."

The empire's profitable commerce in gold is well documented in other sources of the period. Writes one well-traveled Spanish Moor, Abu Hamid al-Andalusi, "In the sands of that country is gold, treasure inexpressible. Merchants trade with salt for it, taking the salt on camels from the salt mines. They start from a town called Sijilmasa and travel in the desert as it were upon the sea, having guides to pilot them by the stars or rocks. They take provisions for six months, and when they reach Ghana they weigh their salt and sell it against a certain unit of weight of gold according to the market and the supply."

Apparently, Ghana's early attempts at controlling the gold supply at its southern source were soon abandoned, since they resulted in an immediate collapse of gold production. Instead, says al-Bakri, the king of Ghana levied a tax, payable only in gold, on all goods traveling into and out of his domain. The king also required that all gold nuggets found within the empire be deposited in royal coffers. Otherwise, explains al-Bakri, "gold would become so abundant as practically to lose its value."

On such wise practices, the Empire of Ghana grew immensely wealthy. Much of this wealth must have gone toward maintaining the empire's complex administrative machinery—its coterie of ministers, governors, and commanders in charge of the empire's vassal states and armies. According to al-Bakri, the king of Ghana commanded an army of 200,000, who pledged military service in exchange for land and trade privileges.

By al-Bakri's day, the empire had established a capital city, possibly in the southeast corner of present-day Mauritania. He describes it as consisting of two towns. In the royal town, the court resided in traditional houses surrounded by a palisade. Nearby, sacred groves sheltered the tombs of past kings, where an elite class of priests still performed what were in this Muslim observer's eyes "pagan" rituals. Some six miles away stood the merchant town, home of the Muslims who plied the trans-Saharan trade. Evidently the traders were a devout lot; the town had 12 mosques.

The archaeological record seems to bear out al-Bakri's testimony. Though the evidence so far obtained is still far from conclusive, excavations conducted during the 1950s and the 1970s in Mauritania by French teams suggest that the merchant quarters of Ghana's capital may lie in the abandoned medieval town of Koumbi Saleh. Within the town's confines, the archaeologists also uncovered a number of two-story stone dwellings whose lower floors were storerooms; these houses were perhaps the abode of al-Bakri's well-heeled merchants. Artifacts found at the site would seem to support such a conclusion: Strewn about were glass weights for measuring gold, fragments of Mediterranean pottery, stones with Arabic inscriptions of Koranic verses, and a particularly fine pair of scissors. The French discovered the ruins of a large mosque in the town's center. From Koumbi Saleh's extensive cemeteries and the close clustering of its houses, they surmised that as many as 20,000 inhabitants may once have resided in the capital.

Archaeologists have so far failed to find any trace of the royal town. Though it remains uncertain that the Ghana capital was razed, it could have been destroyed in 1076 by a Berber Muslim religious sect known as the Almoravids, which ruled Morocco and Spain in the 11th and 12th centuries. They swept into Ghana to avenge the seizure of Awdaghust, a wealthy Berber caravan town some 300 miles northwest of Koumbi Saleh. The Almoravids recaptured Awdaghust and established their brand of Islam as the empire's formal religion.

During this period of confusion and turmoil, the Empire of Ghana began a slow decline. By the second half of the 13th century, the lucrative trans-Saharan trade routes had shifted south and west, bypassing Ghana altogether. The displacement of the old trade network reflected the dispersal of Ghana's peoples, many of whom, to escape the Berber threat, had migrated south. These experienced traders forged new commercial links and founded new merchant states. The most powerful among them, enriched by their control of the gold fields to the south, turned conquering armies on their weaker neighbors. Out of such internecine warfare arose a much larger, richer, and stronger successor to Ghana—the Empire of Mali.

Over the course of its 300-year dominion, Mali grew to encompass the lands ranging westward from the Niger to the Atlantic coast and southward to the gold country of the lower savanna. The empire controlled outposts such as the caravan town of Takedda far to the east and the salt mines of Taghaza in the Sahara Desert.

Ibn Battuta, the peripatetic Muslim scholar, paused in Taghaza in the year 1353, on his caravan journey across the Sahara to the Empire of Mali. From quarries in Taghaza, he watched great slabs of salt being loaded onto waiting camels for export to the interior of Africa. Although a key outpost in Mali's vast merchant network, the town offered little in the way of creature comforts. "This is a village with nothing good about it," records Ibn Battuta. "It is the most fly ridden of places."

Ibn Battuta's memoirs also discuss Mali's prodigious trade in copper—according to the scholar, copper rods doubled as imperial currency. A discovery made in the 1960s deep in the desert of southern Mauritania by the noted French naturalist Theodore Monod dramatizes the perils of the trans-Saharan copper trade. While scouting the desert by camel, Monod and a Bedouin guide came upon an irregular elevation in the sand. Digging down, the two of them uncovered some 2,000 copper rods—still in their carrying baskets—each weighing one pound and measuring two feet long. The rods had been lashed with twine into bundles of 100. Sometime during the 12th century, for reasons unknown, caravanners had dumped this valuable load.

Along with mainstays such as gold, copper, and salt, the Mali empire also operated a diverse commodities market. From

Egypt and North Africa came thoroughbred horses, wool, leather, dried fruit, and olive oil. And from more distant lands in western Europe and Asia appeared textiles, glass, timber, and luxuries such as perfume, Chinese silks, and spices conveyed by caravan across the Sahara Desert. Tiny, lustrous cowrie shells—Mali's favorite medium of small-scale exchange—were gathered off the Maldive Islands in the faraway Indian Ocean.

Like Ghana before it, the Empire of Mali accrued fabulous wealth by controlling the movement of such goods through its realm. Commercial hegemony transformed the city of Timbuktu from a dusty trading depot on the Niger River into one of the most sophisticated and affluent towns in the world at that time. The streets of Timbuktu teemed with caravans laden with exotic goods. Judges, holy men, and merchants dwelled in the town's many-windowed homes and worshiped in its ornate mosques. The literacy rate among its residents was certainly as high as in any European city of the Middle Ages. By the late 15th century, Timbuktu had 150 schools of Koranic studies and was turning a brisk trade in handwritten volumes from North Africa.

In his book of travels, Ibn Battuta described the splendors of an audience with Mali's king at his royal court. The king emerged, writes the scholar, "preceded by his musicians, who carry gold and silver *guimbris* [two-string guitars], and behind him come 300 armed slaves." Clad in a "velvety red tunic" and stepping upon a carpet of silk, the emperor made his way to a platform shaded from the African sun by a large umbrella—"a sort of pavilion made of silk, surmounted by a bird fashioned in gold about the size of a falcon."

The most spectacular evidence of Mali's wealth comes from the reign of one of its greatest kings, Mansa Musa. Like every good Muslim, the king yearned to make a hajj (a pilgrimage to the holy city of Mecca) during his lifetime. Planning a layover in Cairo at the end of the grueling trans-Saharan leg of the journey, Mansa Musa sent a "calling card" to the sultan of Egypt—an emissary bearing 50,000 gold dinars. In 1324 Mansa Musa and his entourage of 8,000—accompanied by 100 pack camels, each loaded with 300 pounds of gold—arrived in the Egyptian capital.

Twelve years later, the king's visit was still recalled with wonder, as reported by Egyptian geographer al-Omari: "This man spread upon Cairo the flood of his generosity: there was no person, officer of the court, or holder of any office of the sultanate who did not re-

ceive a sum of gold from him. The people of Cairo earned incalculable sums from him, whether by buying and selling or by gifts. So
much gold was current in Cairo that it ruined the value of money."

Following the reign of Mansa Musa, a series of inept and increasingly frivolous rulers provoked a cycle of civil wars and coups d'état that
destroyed Mali's fragile unity. East of the Niger Bend, the robust
mercantile city-state of Gao, in the heartland of the Songhay people,
declared independence from Mali in 1375. Into the power vacuum
created by Mali's disintegration the Songhay gradually built a new
empire, which by 1493 encompassed all of central West Africa. Even
Jenné was reduced to vassal status by Songhay's might.

In the village of Sane, near Gao, stand some old tombstones
of Spanish marble engraved with an ancient form of Arabic writing.
"Here lies the tomb of the king who defended God's religion, and
who rests in God, Abu Abdallah Muhammad," reads one stone dat-

*An enthroned Mansa Musa, the fabled
warrior-king of Mali, holds out a golden
nugget to an approaching Saharan merchant in this detail from a 1375 European map of West Africa. Made wealthy
through trade, Mansa Musa's empire
stretched from the Atlantic to the Niger
Bend and from the lucrative trading
centers on the edge of the Sahara to the
fringes of the southern rain forest.*

ed, according to the Islamic calendar, to the year 494 (AD 1100). The inscription confirms that, as early as the 12th century, the kings of Gao had established trade links with Islamic Spain. Certainly, Gao's trading sights had been directed southward as well, toward the gold fields of the coastal forest.

One of Gao's southern contacts may have been Begho, a trade depot founded sometime during the 11th century on a route passing through the Banda Hills, near the Volta River and the entrance to the southern forests in modern-day Ghana. Excavations performed by the British archaeologist Merrick Posnansky during the 1970s revealed that, by the rise of the Songhay empire, Begho had grown to a large city whose handsome mud dwellings were clustered in distinct quarters around a central market. As with many other West Africa communities before Islam became widely accepted, the locals and their chief lived in one quarter and the Muslim traders in another. Begho's blacksmiths and artisans—potters, weavers, and ivory sculptors—were housed separately.

The merchants living in Begho's trade quarter bartered North African goods—Moroccan dresses, glass beads, and brass bowls—for the forest's bounty of gold, kola nuts, ivory, and craftwork, sending these north with slaves who acted as porters along the region's trade routes, probably via Islamic Jenné. A few alien design elements in Begho's locally produced pottery mimic those found in Jenné's ceramicware, indicating a close trade relationship. Strong oral traditions also link the two trading centers. And other artifacts—spindle whorls for yarn making and pottery weights for measuring gold—recall those found in Jenné.

So potent was Begho's standing in the intricate web of West African trade that it would outlast the Songhay empire by several centuries. Like Ghana and Mali before it, Songhay would fall victim to political infighting that left it fragmented and vulnerable to outside aggression. By 1591 the empire was no more, but Begho continued to thrive, thanks to its strong trade connections with the southern forests and the coast.

When Portuguese merchants first arrived on West Africa's shores in the late 15th century, making the lengthy journey in their improved sailing vessels, called caravels, they found some people dressed in Tunisian shawls and Moroccan gowns obtained at inland markets such as Begho in exchange for sea salt and fish. In the years that followed, European goods appeared in the marketplaces, too:

tobacco, Dutch vases, and Venetian glass beads. Archaeologists have so far unearthed more than 1,000 smoking pipes at Begho, as well as fragments of 17th-century Chinese porcelain.

Begho's diverse trade inventory only hints at the complexity of West Africa's southern states. Beneath the forest canopy there flourished civilizations every bit as brilliant as any found in the savanna and the Sahel. But unlike the great empires of Ghana, Mali, and Songhay, most of these societies flowered and passed away unseen by foreign eyes. Their stories are recalled only in the oral traditions of their proud descendants and in the land itself—a silent repository of past glories archaeologists are only now beginning to tap.

Perhaps the most enigmatic of the many tales archaeology has to tell about the forgotten cultures of the West African forest is that of Igbo Ukwu, in modern Nigeria. In 1939, in this small forest village some 25 miles east of the Niger near the head of its ocean delta, Isaiah Anozie was digging a water cistern in the courtyard of his home. About two feet down, his hoe struck a hard object. Wresting it from the soil, Anozie examined his find: a bronze bowl, green with age and fancifully wrought with figures of insects and small animals. Anozie propped the bowl against the wall of his house and continued digging. Soon he came upon another object and then another; before long, he had amassed a hoard of more than 40 similarly wondrous articles, most of which he gave away.

Eventually, some of these found their way into Nigeria's Federal Department of Antiquities, where in 1958 they caught the eye of its British director, Bernard Fagg. Recognizing the artifacts' importance, Fagg recruited the services of Cambridge-trained archaeologist Thurstan Shaw to excavate the site where Anozie had first found them. Shaw arrived in Igbo Ukwu in November 1959 and learned that Anozie's brother, Richard, had also turned up a number of equally striking bronzes on his own property. With only four months remaining before his departure for England, Shaw immediately started excavating both sites, which, appropriately enough, he named Igbo Isaiah and Igbo Richard.

A week into the dig, neither site had yielded much of consequence. The most notable items were an iron blade, a welter of potsherds, and some hearth charcoal. One morning, however, Shaw heard the excited voice of a local helper calling to him from the trenches at Igbo Isaiah. "Something spectacular, sir!" he cried. "Come and see!" Out of one wall of the trench poked the greenish rim of a bronze vessel. It took Shaw the rest of the day to extract the piece. By midafternoon, a large crowd of onlookers had gathered around the site, straining at the surrounding fence for a better look. Carefully chipping at the hardened earth with a wooden tool, Shaw struggled to free the object. Finally, as the light began to fade, he pulled it from its resting place and placed it on a bed of soft paper. Even caked with earth, its magnificence was plain to see.

It was a bronze replica of a water jug encased in a toting net of interlaced bronze rope. Vase, netting, and pedestal had been fashioned in a series of castings—a supreme artistic achievement. Employing the lost-wax method, the smith had first fashioned a wax model of various parts of the object and then coated the forms with a thin veneer of clay to form the molds. When each piece was fired, the encased wax ran out through a tiny hole in the pottery exterior, leaving a hollow into which the artist then poured the molten bronze. After the metal had hardened, the clay jackets were removed. The resulting bronze casts were exact replicas of the wax originals. The artist had then fused the cast segments together by pouring bronze between the seams.

Shaw packed the vase in a cardboard box and covered the dig with a tarpaulin heavily weighted with stones. After assigning a night watchman to the site, he retired, placing the boxed vessel under his bed for safekeeping. This, it turned out, was a sensible precaution; someone entered his office during the night and rifled through his belongings, looking for the vase.

Over the coming days, a sublime cache of artifacts was lifted from the soil of Igbo Isaiah. There were bronze urns chased with beetles and snakes, calabash-shaped bowls, bronze pendant ornaments of elephant and leopard heads, ornamental staffs and swords, and thousands of beads of multicolored glass and red carnelian, a translucent stone. One particularly fine piece, a foot-long shell of bronze, imitated the whorled triton, a mollusk that inhabits coastal waters 100 miles to the south. The shell's pointed end bore a tiny sprinkler, suggesting some ceremonial use. The objects seem to have been laid out on a clay platform that had once been enclosed by a shrine. There they had remained, interred under layers of forest soil.

Shaw, however, had little time to ponder why these articles had been left to the ages. In the nearby plot of Igbo Richard, excavators had come upon still more riveting finds. About six feet down, they encountered a jumbled stash of striped glass beads and copper bangles interspersed with the bone fragments of five persons. Somewhat deeper lay three ivory tusks and a crown of copper, fashioned rather like a tiara. The skull it had once adorned was found close by, shrouded in a mass of bright blue beads; apparently these had once veiled the wearer's face. Nearby rested a semicircular pectoral plate of hammered copper, copper anklets and wristlets, an elephant tusk, and a cast-bronze hilt depicting a horse and rider. The hilt had probably once been attached to a fly whisk, a traditional African symbol of authority.

From a scattering of iron nails and wooden fragments, Shaw deduced that the person had been buried seated on a throne. His mourners had enclosed him in a wooden vault, atop which lay five additional bodies—but whether they were willing or unwilling sacrificial victims no one could say. According to the radiocarbon analysis of a fragment of the wooden throne, the burial had taken place sometime during the ninth century AD.

The early date shocked and baffled archaeologists. Seldom, if ever, had a West African burial revealed such a concentration of wealth in the possession of one man. Even more intriguing were the locally produced copper adornments and cast-bronze artworks whose virtuosity remains unexcelled to this day. That such a rich and artistically advanced culture had reached its apogee at a time when the savanna kingdoms were still young and the trans-Saharan trade routes scarcely developed seemed unthinkable.

Disappointingly, no corroborating dates could be obtained from Igbo Isaiah. But four years later, Thurstan Shaw excavated a third hoard of bronze objects, which was buried in a shallow pit on land abutting Isaiah Anozie's house. In addition to several cast-bronze artworks, the pit yielded four samples of charcoal, three of which were dated to the ninth century. (An anomalous reading of the 15th century from the fourth sample probably represents a later disturbance of the site.)

Researchers have consequently turned from debating the validity of the Igbo Ukwu dates to exploring the nature of the forest society itself. For help in this, Shaw has investigated the oral traditions of the modern Igbo peoples, who still inhabit the forested lands surrounding Igbo Ukwu. The Igbo, he learned, historically organized themselves into self-governing villages headed by family leaders.

Excavations at Igbo Ukwu, a village in eastern Nigeria, have produced one of the great treasures of African art, a unique collection of ornate ritual vessels cast in bronze. Perhaps the most elaborate of the bronzes, this magnificent foot-high pot and stand, encircled by a cage of knotted rope, was probably used for sacred water. It dates from the ninth century AD.

Although these independent hamlets recognized no king, they vested considerable authority in a class of titled priests. By virtue of their ability to promote the land's fertility and shield people from curses, these priests wielded tremendous power. Igbo oral histories recall that certain of these individuals carried elephant tusks carved into horns, which they sounded at the start of all ceremonies. The man buried in the tomb at Igbo Richard, encircled as he was by tusks, may have been such a priest.

The Igbo's oral tradition has nothing to say about the origins of their forebears' bronze-casting knowledge. Until the 1980s, however, many scholars assumed the Igbo had learned it from itinerant North African smiths. But chemical analysis of the alloys that were used in making the Igbo Ukwu bronzes shows that the metal has an unusually high silver content, indicating an indigenous method of production. Arab and European smiths always removed this silver from their molten-bronze products. This suggested that the Igbo Ukwu bronzes represented a local, independently evolved skill.

Archaeologists, though, could find no locally available source of copper—a key component of the bronzes. Then, in 1991, scientists from the University of Nigeria at Nsukka discovered a copper- and lead-mining site in the Benue Rift, only 50 miles to the west of Igbo Ukwu. Charcoal samples taken from old smelting sites in the mine were dated to the ninth century—the same period in which the Igbo Ukwu bronzes are believed to have been cast. Moreover, copper ore from the mine has been found to contain a considerable amount of silver, identical in proportion to the Igbo bronzes.

The lost-wax masterpieces of Igbo Ukwu, then, were conceived and executed by Igbo virtuosos, who developed their own smelting processes more than 1,100 years ago. Extraordinary as it may seem to many people today, however, the Igbo are only part of the larger artistic tradition that has distinguished the region for untold centuries.

One of the greatest flowerings of this creative heritage occurred across the Niger River from Igbo Ukwu, in Ife, the holy province of the Yoruba people. Ife's art, though a few centuries older than Igbo Ukwu's, came to the world's attention first, by nearly 50 years, after Leo Frobenius, an adventurous German ethnographer, visited Ife in 1910.

Frobenius first heard of Ife from a Yoruba sailor who was visiting the port of Hamburg. The sailor told Frobenius of the sacred shrines surrounding the town, where, he said, the deity of wealth and the sea—known in Yoruba as Olokun—was worshiped with great solemnity. Part of the ritual, Frobenius learned, involved digging up the heads of ancestors long since "turned to stone." Intrigued, the ethnographer set out for Ife.

What Frobenius found there disappointed him. The city's shrines were simple tropical groves marked by a few crudely carved stone icons. One day, however, while observing a rite in one of these groves, Frobenius spied "two bits of reddish-brown terracotta embedded in the earth. They were pieces of a broken human face and when I saw these fragments, I grasped the full meaning of what

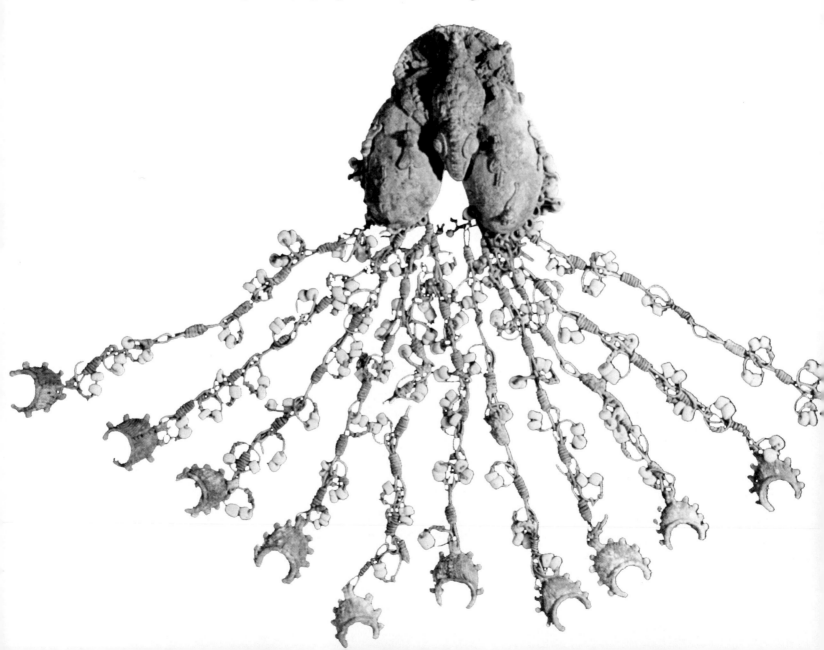

The intricate surface decorations of this bronze triton shell are typical of Igbo artisanship. Surmounted by a leopard on a circular pedestal and covered with jewel-like filigree patterns, the 1,100-year-old vessel likely had ceremonial functions.

A watchful, big-eyed bird broods on top of a pair of oversize eggs in this unusual bronze pendant from Igbo Ukwu. Insects, rare in African art, appear frequently on Igbo bronzes, and three flies alight on each of the eggs. Attached to the back of the pendant are 11 six-inch copper-wire chains decorated with yellow beads and beaklike bronze jingle ornaments.

I had been told. Here were the remains of a very ancient and fine type of art infinitely nobler than the comparatively coarse stone images."

Enthralled by his find, Frobenius and his assistant began tunneling beneath the grove of Olokun. The ethnographer's "burrowings" proved fantastically productive; 18 feet down the excavators were still finding pottery, statuary, and "exquisitely life-like terracotta heads, with clear-cut features and purity of style."

But the best was yet to come. After much prodding, Frobenius persuaded the priest of the Olokun Grove to show him "a head of marvelous beauty, wonderfully cast in antique bronze, true to the life, encrusted with the patina of glorious dark green. This was in very deed, the Olokun, Atlantic Africa's Poseidon." Frobenius purchased the head for six pounds sterling plus a bottle of scotch and a tumbler. When the British district officer got wind of the German scholar's dealings, he declared the sale invalid and forced Frobenius to return the treasure. It later disappeared and was replaced by a forgery; the original has never resurfaced.

In keeping with the Eurocentric prejudices of the age, Frobenius deduced that the artistic brilliance evident in the Olokun Grove had been introduced to West Africa by seafaring peoples from the Mediterranean. Finding no local precedent for such artisanship, the German left Ife convinced that he had found Atlantis, the lost colony of ancient Greece.

In 1943, however, Bernard Fagg, at that time a young British cadet stationed in the Nigerian savanna north of Ife, discovered what many art historians and archaeologists have come to regard as Frobenius's missing precedent. In that year, an engineer at a nearby mine on the Jos Plateau showed Fagg a terra-cotta head that he had purchased from a miner, who had been using it as a scarecrow in his yam field. The laborer had unearthed the piece while digging for tin. It was exceptionally well modeled, with elaborately stylized hair and expressive eyes. An amateur archaeologist, Fagg recognized the head's value. He enlisted the help of other miners in finding more sculptures, which he subsequently designated as belonging to the Nok culture—after the place they were first found (*pages 112-113*).

More than a thousand years divide the Nok and Ife cultures, but some scholars believe that the ancient sculptors of Nok are in some sense the artistic forebears of the peoples of Ife. The

Nok villagers were part of a revolutionary culture that, archaeological evidence shows, was forging iron by the sixth century BC. Materially and artistically advanced, they are likely to have spawned several of the creative, social, and religious practices common to the forest lands to their south.

The British art historian Frank Willet believes that the metamorphosis of the stylized sculpture of Nok tradition into the naturalistic ceramic and bronze sculpture of Ife is chronicled in Yoruba myth. Art historians rely extensively on oral traditions for their interpretations. According to one such tradition, the god Oduduwa descended to Ife—the center of all creation—and became its first ruler, or *oni*. He fathered 16 children, who fanned out from Ife to found the Yoruba states.

Other Yoruba legends hold that Oduduwa came from Mecca or from Egypt. A close study of these accounts has led Willet to conclude that a small but influential group of migrants, probably from the northeast, arrived in Ife around the beginning of the second millennium AD. They brought with them a refined artistic tradition and a knowledge of brass casting, which they taught to the Yoruba, who were already sculpting in terra cotta.

The migrants also introduced the concept of divine kingship, out of which grew myths exalting Ife as the center of the world and the birthplace of the sons of Oduduwa. The kings of Ife's 16 states journeyed to the holy city for their coronations, and pilgrims converged on its sacred groves to lay petitions before the Yoruba gods.

Something of the ancient character of this West African mythological locus was revealed through a series of excavations that began in 1949. Archaeologists were able to infer the placement of Ife's buildings from the town's potsherd courtyards. Laid out in elaborate geometric patterns, the broken pottery and white-quartz pebbles defined the interior spaces and passageways around which had stood houses built of sun-dried mud, with beaten-earth floors. The dwellings, each fringed by its own garden, clustered closely about the palace of the oni at Ife's center.

A series of walls marked the incremental growth of the sacred city from its inception around AD 850 until its decline around the 16th century. In the city's oldest zone, diggers discovered crucibles lacquered with a bluish waste and globules of glass that were later identified as the by-product of bead manufacturing. Glass beads and forest products probably constituted Ife's major exports; the wealth

Portuguese noblemen line the base of this 16th-century ivory salt cellar carved by an artist from Benin, an important trading kingdom in the forests west of the Niger delta. The lid of the 11¾-inch container is capped with a sailing ship complete with crow's nest and club-wielding lookout. Such ivory goods were produced exclusively for European markets and often traded for guns or for brass used in artwork.

these generated, coupled with the rich offerings left at city shrines, sustained Ife's royal court and its superlative arts.

The greatest of Ife's brass sculptures celebrate the oni and his ruling aristocracy. Many of these creations were accidentally unearthed by a workman who was digging outside the confines of the oni's palace in 1938. They depict heads of serene grace and godlike figures that are clothed in beaded robes and clutching magical scepters. More common but no less inspired are the scores of terra-cotta sculptures.

In 1972 the British archaeologist Peter Garlake, working with the University of Ife, carried out an excavation that has given scholars their first insights into the ancient use of these terra-cotta sculptures. Garlake found buried at the center of a 600-year-old potsherd pavement a vessel whose bas-relief design shows three ceramic heads—one a portraitlike bust and the other two cone-shaped—standing together in a thatched shrine. Surrounding the shrine are images of ritual objects: a drum, a dagger, a pair of cow horns, and a human corpse upside down in a basket.

Within a few feet of this find Garlake unearthed several iron nails whose position suggested the presence of a long-vanished timber building. At its center lay a pile of broken terra-cotta statuary and bone fragments of human limbs and torsos. Nearby was a heap of 40 human skulls. Whether these were the victims of sacrifice remains unclear. Certainly, however, the spot had been the focus of some sort of ceremonial devotion.

By the 15th century the Yoruba of Ife saw their wealth and influence begin to dwindle as competing forest states usurped important trade routes and consolidated their power. Of these rivals, Benin—a city-state of the Edo people 100 miles to Ife's southeast—eventually became the greatest. (Ancient Benin lay entirely within Nigeria and did not encompass the modern Republic of Benin.)

Benin's ascendancy began in 1440 with the reign of Ewuare the Great. According to Edo oral traditions, Ewuare—the oba, or king—was a direct descendant of Oduduwa, the first oni of Ife. Like Oduduwa, Ewuare was considered divine; so potent was his gaze that the oba was obliged to wear a beaded veil over his face to shield onlookers from his awesome power. He is remembered as a maker of "powerful charms," a doctor, a warrior, a musician, and a sagacious ruler. Credited with capturing 201 towns and villages, Ewuare vastly increased Benin's wealth and transformed it from a royal city-state into a true kingdom.

To enclose his palace, Ewuare commanded the building of Benin's formidable inner wall—a seven-mile-long earthen rampart girdled by a moat some 50 feet deep—which was excavated in the early 1960s by the British archaeologist Graham Connah. Connah estimates that construction of the wall, if spread out over five dry seasons, would have required a force of 1,000 laborers working 10 hours a day, seven days a week. But this was not Ewuare's only public-works project; he also added great thoroughfares to the city and erected nine fortified gateways. Subsequent excavations have revealed something even more amazing—a rural network of earthen walls some 4,000 to 8,000 miles in length, which would have taken an estimated 150 million man-hours to construct and hundreds of years to complete. These were apparently thrown up as a means of demarcating territories belonging to different towns and cities.

Only 13 years after Ewuare's death, in 1473, tales of Benin's splendors lured Portuguese merchants from their coastal trading posts to the city's gates. They were soon followed by the British, the Dutch, and the Florentines, all of whom came to Benin seeking pepper, gold, ivory, and slaves. Tempted by the exotic wares displayed before them—velvets, firearms, candied fruits, saddles, gilded mirrors—the acquisitive Edo quickly forged a trade relationship with the Europeans. According to one Dutch merchant, the oba's agents came down to the port "magnificently dressed, wearing necklaces of jasper or fine coral."

After greeting the European merchants and presenting them with luscious fruits from the oba's groves, the Edo would get down to bargaining—"sometimes for whole months." The shrewdness of the Edo merchants prompted the British trader Richard Eden to write in 1590: "They are a very wary people in their bargaining, and will not lose one sparke of golde of any value. They use weights and measures, and are very circumspect in occupying the same." The Edo's business acumen won them fantastic riches. At the kingdom's height during the 16th century, Benin City may have housed as many as 60,000 people, who, it was said, hailed each other with the salutation, "Thank God, what wealth has done for me!"

PROMOTING THE POWER OF THE OBA OF BENIN IN PLAQUES OF BRASS

"Whoever wants to succeed in life should not heed the bird that cries disaster." So declared Oba Esigie, 16th-century king of Benin, when an ibis bird supposedly predicted his defeat in a war with the Igala people. He had the ibis killed and went on to defeat the Igala. It was audacity typical of a divine oba of Benin—and an event worth recording on one of the wall plaques adorning the palace.

Since at least the reign of Esigie, Benin kings had commissioned small brass plaques—generally about a foot and a half high—to celebrate significant events and traditions from the city-state's royal past. Except to wage war or take part in annual religious ceremonies, the king rarely appeared in public, and such decorations were one way to perpetuate his all-powerful image before the people. With royal patronage, Benin became a major center for brass casting

in West Africa, using zinc and copper obtained from trade with the Portuguese during the 16th and 17th centuries. The elaborate rectangular plaque reliefs—rare in African art—may well have been influenced by illustrated books brought by European merchants.

Nailed to great wooden pillars that supported the palace roof, the embossed plaques proclaimed the king's power—over death, war, and nature.

But forces greater than the absolute monarch of Benin were closing in on the forest kingdom. The British Punitive Expedition entered the city in 1897, the first enemy to do so. By this time the brass plaques were no longer on display but were instead packed away in a palace storehouse. Hundreds of the reliefs were shipped abroad, war trophies for the victors. And so ended the power of the now-exiled oba of Benin.

A triumphant Oba Esigie and two of his attendants return to Benin City after their victory in the Igala war of 1515. The warrior on the left carries an effigy of an oracular ibis, a bird that had predicted Esigie would be defeated at the hands of the Igala. With his unexpected triumph, the king had not only beaten an external enemy and increased the size of his kingdom; he had seemingly overcome fate itself.

Flanked supportively by two attendants with leopards at their feet, this king of Benin is depicted with mudfish for legs, identifying him with Olokun, deity of the great waters and the source of all worldly wealth. The plaque may also recall a king from the early 15th century, Oba Ohen, whose legs had become paralyzed; he was often depicted with mudfish legs to hide the deformity that would have excluded him from the throne.

This stylized human figure is a representation of Ofoe, messenger of Ogiwu, the god of death. Mounted on the palace walls, such a plaque declared the oba's authority over life and death throughout his realm.

Shaded from the sun by two attendants holding up their shields, a Benin oba sits sidesaddle on his horse, a manner of riding reserved exclusively to the king. Smaller figures, sword-bearers, ceremonially support the king's outstretched hands, symbolizing that even he ruled with the sanction of the people. The varying sizes of the figures indicate their relative status within the hierarchical court of Benin.

In a demonstration of his power over the animals of the wild, a mudfish-legged oba swings two leopards by the tails in this bronze plaque. Leopards were sacrificed at the oba's coronation and during annual ceremonies designed to enhance the god-king's mystical powers.

Nowhere was this wealth more conspicuous than in the palace of the oba. A maze of apartments and galleries arranged around more than 100 courtyards, the palace took up, as a Dutch visitor wrote, "as much space as the town of Haarlem," with most of the galleries as "big as those on the Exchange of Amsterdam." Covering its ceilings and wooden timbers were cast brass plaques depicting war exploits and ceremonial life. Within each court, richly ornamented altars displayed bronze portrait heads surmounted by carved ivory tusks. Here, the oba and his minions performed rites designed to harmonize relations between Benin's ancestors and the spirit realm. Some involved dressing the bronzes with coral beads and dousing them with the blood of human sacrifice. Only by such extreme measures, the Edo believed, could they ensure the kingdom's welfare.

By the late 18th century, such appeals ceased to be enough. The very riches that had lofted Benin to the height of prosperity now plunged it toward ruin. Out of the kingdom's solid union arose rebel states—armed with European flintlocks—bent on seizing a larger share of the region's trade. As the kingdom fell into chaos, the oba and his retinue withdrew deeper into the palace confines, shunning all contact with Europeans and the renegades.

Within a century Benin—once a vast kingdom that included many of the forest states west of the Niger—was reduced to an enclave surrounding Benin City. The final, catastrophic blow came not at the hands of the disenchanted people but from outsiders who had once conducted peaceful, mutually beneficial relations with Benin.

In 1897 the British made repeated overtures to the oba about reopening trade. When these were rebuffed, the British acting consul general set off on an uninvited visit to the palace. Unbeknown to the oba, two Edo chiefs arranged to ambush the consul general and his party, killing seven of the nine Europeans and most of the 200 Africans. Fearful of a reprisal, the oba embarked on an appalling campaign of ritual slaughter, sacrificing hundreds of human victims in the hopes of winning protection for the city.

The oba's efforts were in vain. The forces of the British Punitive Expedition entered Benin City on February 18, 1897. The town, a gory sepulcher, stood deserted. One of the British entered the palace and left a vivid description of what he saw. "The big door," he wrote, "is lined with sheets of brass with stamped figures of men and leopards' heads. On the other side of the compound the wall is partly roofed in, and along this is a row of brass heads,

The University of Dakar's Hamady Bocoum (top right), *one of Africa's leading archaeologists, oversees a 1990 excavation at a site along the Middle Senegal Valley that predates the region's earliest-recorded empires. Bocoum is part of a new generation of African archaeologists determined to discover their peoples' history.*

and on top of every head is a long, heavy weather-worn finely carved ivory tusk. Between the brass heads were brass castings of men on horseback, in armour, in chain mail. All the articles were thickly encrusted with blood, and a fearful smell pervaded the place. Through this compound is the king's meeting house. The first thing that strikes you here is the metal roof on which, just facing you, is an immense brass snake crawling down with its big head close to the gutter. All the rafters have been covered with brass sheeting on which figures have been punched. The roof is supported by over one hundred pillars of bronze sheets riveted together, giving a very good effect."

From the grounds of the palace, British troops removed some 2,000 pieces of priceless Benin art. One member of the Punitive Expedition, writing some years later, praised the pieces, some of which he could identify as having been produced in the 16th century. "There was no such high-class art in the Iberian peninsula at the end of the 15th century; and we know that there was not much of this art in the rest of Europe."

Taken to Britain as spoils of war, the objects were auctioned off to help pay for the cost of the foray and to set up pensions for its members and the kin of those who had died. The oba was forced into exile. After his death in 1914, his son was brought back to Benin by the British and installed as oba. The coral beads that had been worn by each succeeding ruler as a sign of royal dignity and power were returned to him. As part of his effort to restore the burned-out palace, the new oba commissioned brass plaques and ivory objects to replace those taken by the British and had them set on the royal altars so that the ancient Benin rituals could be revived.

Benin was the last of the great forest kingdoms to retain its independence; the era of colonialism was well underway. West Africa was carved up by the great European powers of the day into a hodgepodge of enclaves whose borders made no sense in the age-old context of African society. Ancient enemies were sometimes thrown together under the same colonial administration, while elsewhere ethnic groups were split in two by the new borders. This sad epoch of foreign domination would last into the second half of the 20th century, until new African states—still sometimes awkwardly delineated by colonial boundaries rather than traditional ones—would begin to attain their independence, in some cases peaceably, in others only with prolonged bloodshed.

West Africa's heritage of achievement and greatness was never forgotten by its people. Oral history has passed the record on from parent to child over countless generations. And fortunately, the contemporary states of the region are demonstrating an increasing interest in archaeological exploration, turning to the legacy of the past to help build a sense of national pride in the present and the future. In 1991, for example, Alpha Oumar Konaré supplanted years of destructive military dictatorship to become the first democratically elected president of Mali. He is an archaeologist by training, and his ascendancy not only will facilitate efforts by Western researchers such as the McIntoshes but could also inspire young Malians to follow in his footsteps. It would be a welcome development indeed if West Africans themselves had more opportunity to expand the rest of the world's awareness of their remarkable history.

OUT OF THE AFRICAN EARTH

S tumbling upon fragments of a terra-cotta head, in 1910, that were embedded in the Nigerian earth, the German ethnographer Leo Frobenius instantly saw in the work something remarkable and vastly exciting. Here, Frobenius would write, are "a symmetry, a vitality, a delicacy of form directly reminiscent of ancient Greece."

Since then other similarly impressive works produced in brass, bronze, and ivory, as well as in terra cotta, have been extracted from Nigerian soil. While some of them are highly stylized, others are strikingly realistic, such as the one above, which displays the kind of ornamental scarification many people underwent during rites of passage.

The works in this picture essay come from three different cultures and are separated by centuries, yet similarities among them suggest that they may have been inspired by a common tradition. Even the earliest sculptures—dating to about 500 BC—exhibit great

aesthetic sophistication and technical facility. This leads scholars to believe that all these pieces were the outcome of a long artistic evolution whose beginnings have yet to be traced.

Much of what can be said about the purpose of the sculptures comes from the oral traditions of Nigerians who are living today. Exhibiting the dress and bearing of royalty, many of the pieces doubtless were commissioned by kings, who might have used such art to legitimize their sovereignty. The works may have been given, for example, to appointed officials as badges of authority.

Some of the brass heads are crowned, while others have holes to suggest that real crowns were once attached. The heads, in turn, may have been fixed to wooden bodies. Such figures could have served as funeral effigies, with the detachable crowns a clear indicator that though an individual king may have died, royal authority was passed on.

THE RIDDLE OF NOK SCULPTURE

The earliest of the Nigerian sculptures belong to the Nok culture, so named after the village where the first examples turned up. Since then more than 150 terracotta pieces have been recovered —some from tin-dredging operations—in the Benue River valley, washed there apparently by past floods. Their origin is not known, but it would seem likely that they once adorned shrines, graves, or other sacred settings. Often only heads survive.

Radiocarbon tests performed on wood found in the sculpture-bearing strata show that the Nok culture existed from the fifth century BC to about AD 200. This period precedes the rise of central rule by kings in Nigerian history. People lived then in small ethnic groups that were dispersed throughout the area.

While these highly stylized pieces probably are not the expression of a single such group, most share similar bold characteristics, such as elongated skulls, striking hair styles, and expressive eyes. They are thought to represent ancestors or mythical beings and to have been employed in fertility rites.

The scalp of a bearded man (above) *is shaven, leaving only a single ridge of hair across the top. The hair is styled in a pattern similar to the one applied to the left side of the face between eye and eyebrow. The pierced pupils, nostrils, ears, and mouth, typical of Nok sculpture, are air vents to prevent cracking as the clay hardened during firing.*

An elaborate coiffure arranged in tiers sets off this fifth-century BC Nok head. Some scholars suggest that such an elaborate hairdo indicates a person of high status; others believe that hair styles identify various kinship groups.

Once part of a life-size statue, this head is one of the largest of the Nok pieces yet discovered. Its triangular-shaped eyes are dramatically set off by the arched eyebrows. The buns of hair have holes on top, which once may have been used to hold feathers. Spanning the upper portion of the forehead is a decorative piece that cannot be clearly identified. Archaeologists speculate that it may portray three strands of beads, plaited fiber, or even an iron chain.

LIFELIKE FIGURES OF IFE

While Nok pieces are stylized, the sculptures of Ife, capital of the Yoruba people of southwestern Nigeria, are naturalistic. Indeed, some of them portray human deformity or malevolence. The oldest ones were molded of terra cotta in the seventh century AD. By the 11th century AD artists had begun producing portraits of kings in brass and sometimes in pure copper, using the lost-wax method. To do this, they first had to sculpt their subjects in wax, then coat the models in clay. When heated, the wax would melt and run out through a hole. Into the empty mold the sculptors would pour the molten metal. After the metal cooled, they would break open the mold to reveal the sculpture.

The delicate features of a queen (above) *portrayed in brass are enhanced by parallel scarification marks. Rings like those circling the neck are worn for adornment even today in some parts of Nigeria.*

Limbs are missing from this seated male statue, created in the Ife naturalistic style. It is made of almost pure copper, which is hard to cast because it oxidizes quickly when molten. Believed to have been used in fertility rites, the statue apparently was taken often to the riverbank, where it was scrubbed with gravel, leaving its surface pitted.

The royal couple portrayed at right is digni-
fied in demeanor and dressed regally—from
the tops of their heads to their ankles—in
robes, beads, pendants, and other jewelry. The
double bows on the beaded bibs are insignias
of high rank. The entwined arms and legs
symbolize the joint power of these rulers, who
could be husband and wife, brother and sis-
ter, or mother and son. The proportions of the
two heads—each is approximately a quarter
to a third of the size of the rest of the body—
are typical of Ife statuary.

PRIDE OF THE BINI KINGS

The Bini of southern Nigeria apparently regarded the most capable of their monarchs as divine beings. Accordingly, after rendering sculptures of these obas in wood, terra cotta, brass, and ivory, the Bini placed the effigies on altars that were dedicated to individual deceased kings and worshiped them. Although they stood for particular rulers, the sculptures are nevertheless stylized and do not exhibit individualized features.

Benin has been a kingdom since AD 1100. According to its oral history, brass casting was introduced in the 14th century AD by an oba who wanted to produce works similar to those of Ife. He brought a craftsman by the name of Iguegbae from Ife to Benin to teach Bini artisans the lost-wax method. Once they had mastered the technique, their work fell directly under the control of kings, who had the sole right to commission pieces.

The brass head of a queen mother, or iyoba, *above shows her high rank, for she was the only person besides the king and the chief warrior allowed to wear a crown of coral beads. Hers covers her hair, swept up in the so-called chicken's-beak style. The sculpture probably stood on an altar in the royal palace dedicated to the veneration of high-ranking female ancestors. The iyoba advised the oba and enjoyed a social position equal to that of town chiefs.*

Portrayed in brass, this oba wears multiple collars of coral beads and stone called odigba *around his neck. His face, with swelling cheeks, is capped by a crown beaded in a crisscross pattern and decorated further with clusters of cylindrical beads; from its rim, other beads hang singly and in strands and braids. Pupils of inlaid iron peer from heavily outlined eyes. A particular style of crown was sometimes associated with a certain oba.*

The carved ivory mask of a queen mother at right may have been worn by a king at his left hip, following tradition. The face is framed by a tiara and a neckpiece displaying heads of Portuguese traders, who were associated with the sea gods. Such decoration might have symbolized the oba's far-reaching mercantile connections, based on control of his region's ivory, which he traded for such overseas products as silks and mirrors.

CITIES OF STONE AND CORAL, BUILT ON GOLD

There were the usual rumors of gold and other buried treasure, but E. S. J. van Graan could only imagine what he might find atop the sandstone outcrop known as Mapungubwe, "Hill of the Jackals." Such rumors were as unreliable as the rainy season in some parts of southern Africa. All the farmer and prospector could know for certain, as he clawed his way up the narrow draw that led to the summit, was what local legend had told him: This hill was a place sacred to the Great Ones, so sacred that the people dwelling in the area would neither point at it nor face in its direction when speaking of it.

Spurred by visions of riches, van Graan, a white resident of South Africa, had spent the previous six years pursuing every lead in an effort to pinpoint the location of the consecrated peak. Now, as 1932 drew to a close, he had at last reached his goal, thanks to a local inhabitant who—albeit reluctantly—divulged the location of the rock chimney that formed Mapungubwe's secret ascent.

Scrambling to the top, van Graan, his son, and three companions found themselves surrounded by a jumble of boulders, the larger ones teetering atop the smaller, the whole artifice apparently intended to be tumbled onto the heads of intruders by the long-vanished guardians of the hill. Potsherds, glass beads, bits of copper, and scraps of ancient iron tools littered the summit. But of greater

This modern door in Zanzibar, Tanzania, continues a tradition dating to the early Middle Ages. Swahili artisans adopted the Arab practice of carving wooden door-frames, incorporating such motifs as the leaves, flowers, and chains seen here.

interest to van Graan's party was a piece of gleaming yellow metal pulled from a deposit of eroded soil at the base of a slope. By the next day the treasure seekers had recovered large quantities of gold from the hilltop, including loot ripped from a burial site. They then hastily divided the spoils, going so far as to hack a gold-sheathed rhinoceros figurine into equal shares.

At this point, Mapungubwe seemed destined to join the long list of important African historical sites that were "discovered" by Europeans, only to be desecrated and plundered. Happily for later researchers, however, the younger van Graan suffered an attack of conscience. He had once been a student of the eminent archaeologist Leo Fouchë, at the University of Pretoria, and decided to inform his former professor of the find. By June of 1933 Mapungubwe had been placed under the protection of the South African government, and the first of a series of excavations had already been completed at the site.

At the height of its power in the 12th century AD, Mapungubwe had been the economic and political capital of a sophisticated African state. Though it derived much of its wealth from farming and cattle raising, it was also involved in a lucrative trade network that stretched 400 miles from the Limpopo River valley to the shores of the Indian Ocean.

Ivory was the town's most valuable commodity, and as long

Reassembled from fragments unearthed at Mapungubwe in South Africa, this gold-plated rhinoceros is believed to date from the 12th century AD. Originally, the gold was tacked to a wood or resin core, which has disappeared. One curious aspect of the 5½-inch figurine is its lone horn: African rhinos have two horns, so the artifact could be an import from India, home of the one-horned variety.

as ivory remained in demand by East African merchants to sell to their overseas trading partners, Mapungubwe thrived. But the gold that was found by van Graan—dated to around AD 1200, which makes it the earliest recovered from a site on the Zimbabwe Plateau—points to a shift in taste. Its presence in a burial this early suggests that the metal was already being revered for the status it conferred. People who could afford to take something so precious to the grave must have been rich; perhaps they were the traders who had prospered in their dealings with the Swahili on the east coast. It would be the growing lust for gold—not just by affluent Africans, but by Arab and Mediterranean merchants as well—that would eventually leave Mapungubwe, removed as it was from the gold fields to the north and from the ports through which gold passed, at a geographical disadvantage and set the stage for the rise of the Zimbabwe state.

Indeed, the history of this portion of medieval southern Africa is a story of one state rising at the expense of another, as each jockeyed for access to the trading cities on the East African coast. This competition was mirrored in the cities themselves, which vied to supply merchants from across the Indian Ocean and the Red Sea with ever more gold. When the Portuguese muscled in on the gold trade during the 16th century, they sowed the seeds of destruction by cutting out the middlemen and disrupting the historic networks that linked the interior with the coast in an effort to control the sources of the metal itself.

Until the appearance of the Europeans, however, control of the African gold trade remained firmly in the hands of the Africans themselves—specifically the Swahili merchants. The word *Swahili* means coast dwellers, but so far-flung and pervasive was the trading network that even today the Swahili language is the lingua franca of commerce among Africans dwelling as far west as Zaire. Ethnically, the term refers to a cultural pattern rather than an individual group; geographically, it applies to a narrow strip of coast, dubbed the Swahili Corridor by the British archaeologist Mark Horton. Here, according to Horton, along an 1,800-mile stretch that runs from present-day Somalia southward to Mozambique and includes the Comoro Islands and the northern tip of Madagascar, the sea-trading society that would become known as Swahili took root, perhaps as early as the first century AD.

An official report from that time on Indian Ocean traffic, probably written by an agent of imperial Rome, gives evidence of African coastal trade functioning as part of a wider network. Even at this early date, the exchange of goods between East African markets and those in India and down the coast of southern Arabia was so routine that the author writes of "daily runs" by Indian and Arabian vessels along African ports of call. Imports and exports are also duly noted, with African traders swapping ivory, rhinoceros horn, and tortoiseshell for glassware, iron tools, and weapons.

Ptolemy's second-century *Guide to Geography* provides another intriguing, but often incomplete, picture of commercial traffic plying the Indian Ocean. In recent decades, archaeology has begun to fill in the gaps in the historical record. Excavations at Ras Hafun,

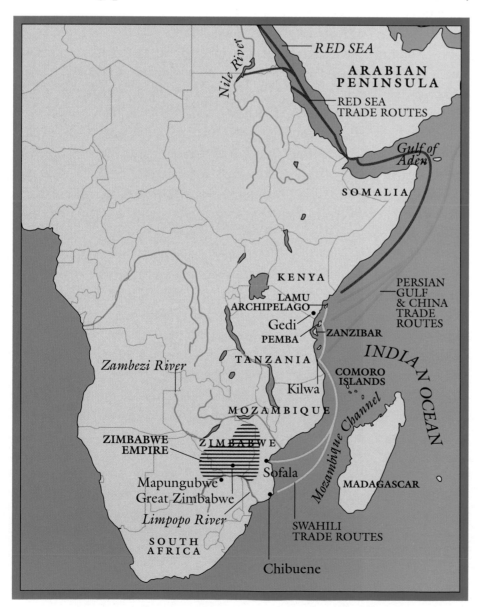

Perhaps as early as the fourth century AD, Indian Ocean merchants began trading with East Africa at sites just south of the horn (green routes). Africans living on the east coast had apparently been navigating its waters for centuries and established mercantile contacts inland. When Arabs from the Red Sea region (purple routes) picked up the trade in the 10th century, the preexisting Swahili network (yellow routes) provided a way to move gold from Zimbabwe (shaded area) and ivory and other products up the coast to northern markets and to various Indian Ocean destinations.

a peninsula just south of the Horn of Africa in present-day Somalia, have produced a variety of ceramics, including imports from Persia, dating from the first century BC to the fifth century AD. Similar finds far to the south at Unguja Ukuu (on the island of Zanzibar, off the coast of Tanzania) and at Chibuene (in southern Mozambique) provide further evidence of a vigorous and expanding trade network. Also at Unguja Ukuu, sherds of locally made pottery of a type normally recovered from mainland sites have been unearthed by a Zanzibari archaeologist by the name of AdbulRaham Juma; they date to the early half of the first millennium, pointing to the early origins of this African settlement.

By the ninth century the Swahili had already solidified their commercial position as middlemen and had begun the cultural metamorphosis that would transform the coast of East Africa into a stronghold of Islam. The exact course of that transformation has been a source of controversy among historians and archaeologists. Until the 1980s most researchers subscribed to the theory, promulgated by the British archaeologist Neville Chittick, that the Swahili were the descendants of Arab merchants who had colonized the East African coast and its offshore islands between the seventh and the 10th century. These Arabs, Chittick wrote, had subsequently intermarried with the indigenous Bantu-speaking farmers, and in time the transplanted Arabic civilization absorbed enough African influences to produce the hybrid Swahili culture.

Local oral traditions, however, suggest that although some Arab merchants did visit coastal cities during this period and decided to stay, such immigration appears to have been on a small scale, and the newcomers themselves were quickly and completely assimilated into the larger Swahili society. Archaeology at numerous sites during the 1980s and the 1990s seems to confirm this: Excavations have revealed traces of earlier African fishing and farming communities under the supposed Arab ruins and tremendous continuity between all the historic phases of the sites. As a result, a new school of thought contends that the Swahili, in the normal course of doing business with the outside world, had adopted the religion and some of the customs of their Arab trading partners and, over time, had given them a uniquely African flavor.

The Swahili were certainly not the first people in the world to adopt foreign traditions in order to, as least partly, facilitate business dealings. And since the ruling elite stood to profit the most from

123

closer ties with its Arab partners in the Indian Ocean trade, it was this segment of Swahili society that first converted to Islam, beginning in the ninth century. The archaeological record of Swahili towns, including the remains of mosques large enough for only a handful of worshipers, would seem to bear this out.

But Islam was attractive to the Swahili for more than just reasons of perceived commercial advantage. It was a written religion that offered a code of ethics and laws. It also offered a unity of spirit with a much wider segment of human society while allowing the Swahili to still maintain their African culture. Consequently, by the 12th century a broad-based acceptance of Islam had taken place in Swahili society, a fact that was reflected in the construction of larger and more numerous mosques.

Of course, conversion to Islam alone would have carried little weight with Arab merchants had the Swahili not been able to deliver the goods. Accordingly, even in pre-Islamic days the Swahili had assiduously developed harbors, pioneered offshore routes, and perfected navigation techniques that were well-suited to the monsoon-driven winds and currents of the coastal waters (such as the treacherous Mozambique Channel between Madagascar and the mainland). The Swahili sailed up and down the coast, in the words of one historian, "as though it were a network of roads," ferrying ivory, gold, and other African products northward and returning home with cloth, glassware, pottery, and other manufactured goods.

It was no small measure of the Swahili's success as traders that, by the ninth century, their "corridor" had been fully integrated into a truly international trade network, which linked East Africa to ports as far away as China. The Swahili had also turned their business talents to inland trade, tapping into existing routes and making themselves the indispensable conduit from the interior to the overseas markets.

All this is not to say that the Swahili were immune to inevitable fluctuations in supply and demand. In fact, by the 10th century they found themselves in an economic downturn triggered by political events in far-off Mesopotamia. There, the draining of salt marshes had created a robust market for African slaves, which the Swahili had been quick to capitalize on. But demand dropped sharply in the wake of the so-called Zanj Revolt, a massive slave uprising that dragged on for 15 years in the latter half of the ninth century. Not long afterward, the end of the Tang dynasty in China precipitated an era of political instability that had a similarly disastrous effect on the demand for ivory.

The Swahili's fortunes rebounded in the mid-10th century, when the demand for new commodities attracted new customers, specifically merchants from the Red Sea and the Gulf of Aden. Those merchants, in turn, offered access to new markets in the Mediterranean. The ivory trade revived, and now also much desired were rock crystal—prized as a carving material by Mediterranean artisans—and gold, which the Swahili themselves had very little use for but which would propel them to greatness in the coming centuries.

The story of the Swahili's economic ups and downs emerges at excavation sites all along the East African coast, where archaeologists have uncovered the ruins of more than 400 settlements, some dating to the eighth century. Missing from the archaeological tale, however, are a few historically recorded sites that have yet to be located. Of those, none has proved more elusive than Rhapta. Named for the area's wooden sailboats, whose planks were lashed together with rope made from palm fiber, Rhapta functioned as a major ivory export center as early as the first century AD. Rhapta was also "the last mainland market town" on the East African coast, according to a Roman report—and thus the end of the known world from the Roman perspective. "Beyond it, the unexplored ocean curves round towards the west."

Ptolemy's *Guide to Geography* adds a few more pieces to the puzzle, noting that by the middle of the second century, Rhapta had become a "metropolis." Citing clues found in both sources, some scholars believe that the lost city probably lies somewhere along a 35-mile stretch of the Tanzanian coastline around Bagamoyo and Dar es Salaam. Others disagree, pointing to a number of discrepancies in the two ancient accounts. A few experts surmise that rather than identifying a single port, the name Rhapta referred to any number of harbors where the sewn boats were found and where sailors could await the inevitable change in the monsoon winds.

Of those sites that have been found, some of the most fascinating lie in the Lamu archipelago, a cluster of low-lying sandy islands near the equator, just off the coast of Kenya. Swahili settlements dating to the eighth century have been discovered on the

With its square, upright sail made of coconut matting, the distinctive mtepe *carried Swahili merchants on their coastal trading voyages from about the first century AD to the early 20th century. Built without nails—the timbers were sewn together with rope made from coconut husks—the mtepe had a prow designed to resemble a camel's head, complete with an eye painted on each side.*

main islands of Lamu, Manda, and Pate. In 1966, at the ruins of the once-prosperous Swahili town of Manda, Neville Chittick began the digs that eventually led to his now-disputed conclusion that "the creation of this town was due to the settling of immigrants who came from the Persian/Arabian Gulf."

Neville Chittick based his belief on a variety of evidence, most notably an unusually large quantity of broken imported pottery of the ninth and 10th centuries. He also claimed to have discovered ample evidence of foreign building techniques, employing stone, that had been in use from the earliest period of occupation. Finally, Chittick drew attention to the massive sea walls that surrounded the site, noting that they and their mode of construction were "without parallel on the East African coast."

But there was one glaring discrepancy in Chittick's theory: If Manda had been an Arab colony since its inception, why had its residents waited until the 14th century—some 500 years later—to build a mosque? That vexing question led fellow archaeologist Mark Horton to challenge what he called Chittick's "model of Asiatic colonization." Horton also maintained that Chittick had misread the evidence at Manda. The presence of so much imported pottery, for example, might merely imply a taste for foreign luxuries on the part of the resident Swahili. He pointed out that Chittick had discovered the imported ceramics in an excavation along the Manda beach, where, as Horton noted, "the imports were unloaded from the long sea voyage and the broken crocks would have been discarded." In such circumstances, an unusually high concentration of foreign pottery would hardly have been unusual.

Horton likewise took issue with Chittick's claim that the residents of Manda had always lived in stone and brick houses. He suggested instead that the pattern established at other East African sites, where stone gradually supplanted more perishable timber and clay, had in all likelihood also prevailed at Manda. Horton's own examination of the evidence convinced him that the town had been

Indirect trade between China and East Africa began as early as the eighth century AD, by way of the Persian Gulf. Porcelain artifacts, such as this 16th-century Ming bowl (above) found near Kunduchi in Tanzania, have been unearthed all along the Swahili coast, and houses, mosques, and pillar tombs, such as the one shown at top, often incorporate the fine ware as decoration. The Chinese received, in turn, various African items, including a Kenyan giraffe seen in the 15th-century silk painting at right.

built by Swahili artisans using indigenous building methods and locally quarried or manufactured materials, particularly porites coral. Cut from underwater reefs, the coral was quickly shaped into rectangular blocks while still wet and soft. The techniques needed to work this kind of material were common in coastal towns along the Red Sea, an indication that the impetus for its use may have come from southern Arabia, together with certain architectural styles. Of Manda's enormous sea walls, Horton did admit that they were, indeed, unique to the African coast and similar to walls found in southern Arabia. Nevertheless, that particular point contributed little to the argument over Manda's origins.

In the end, Horton proposed a revised chronology for the town, contending that as early as AD 800—decades before Chittick's earliest occupation date—Manda was already a thriving community, exporting timber and slaves to the Middle East. Moreover, according to Horton, Manda had never been anything but an African community and had only later absorbed the teachings of Islam. "The archaeological evidence," wrote Horton, "shows how first material culture, then architecture, and finally religion itself was grafted from the Islamic world onto the East African coast."

Mark Horton's refutation of Neville Chittick's findings resulted not only from an examination of Manda but also from Horton's own excavations at Shanga on nearby Pate Island, the largest in the Lamu archipelago. Over six digging seasons, beginning in 1980, Horton uncovered traces of a community that had been continuously occupied from about AD 750 until the early 15th century. During this time, Shanga evolved from a typically African village of the period into a mostly Muslim town of 500, with trading contacts from the Mediterranean to China.

Horton dug down through some 15 feet

of deposits to expose no fewer than 30 distinct occupation phases. The lowest layer furnished evidence of an eighth-century AD village—complete with a rectangular cattle enclosure—of wattle-and-daub houses, which were probably arranged according to membership in clans. The remains of an ancient well were found at the center of the enclosure.

Upper layers of the excavation pit revealed a succession of eight small wooden mosques, each built on the ruins of its predecessor, and all dating from the late eighth to the 10th century. These wooden structures, in turn, formed the footing for a similar succession of stone mosques, the earliest erected in the 10th century and the latest still in use when Shanga was abandoned around 1425.

Horton read these layers the way others read books. They told him the story of Shanga's long and gradual transformation into an Islamic community. As elsewhere in the Swahili Corridor, it probably began with the conversion of the town's ruling elite, as evidenced by the very limited capacity of the first wooden mosque. The new religion did not fully involve the general population for another 200 years, by which time the construction of a large stone mosque indicates that Islam had become predominant.

As Horton also observed, each successive mosque showed an increasingly accurate orientation toward Mecca, suggesting that subsequent builders had benefited from advances in geographical knowledge. He also discovered 100 well-preserved silver coins, the earliest found at a level predating AD 900, the majority dating to about 1000, most of which bear inscribed references to Allah.

The coins also illuminated the close trade links between Shanga and the outside world, since these particular pieces of silver, while apparently minted locally, were in all likelihood copies of Mediterranean coins. One of the coins even bore a name and a rhyming couplet on its reverse side, a formula common to currency minted by the Fatimid caliphs of Sicily. In fact, five silver coins that had actually been minted in Sicily during the 10th and 11th centuries were discovered on nearby Manda Island—further indicating to Horton that "the Swahili rulers of the Lamu archipelago possessed coins from the Mediterranean and were using them as models for minting their own."

To archaeologists, the minting of coins is also a sure sign of growing economic strength. So, too, is building with stone. Shortly after completing its first stone mosque, Shanga flexed its economic

Workers study the earliest evidence of Islam in sub-Saharan Africa at Shanga, Pate Island, off Kenya. English-Kenyan teams headed by Mark Horton unearthed, among other things, groups of postholes from successive wooden mosques dating from AD 800. The small holes here mark the first mosque, the medium-size holes of the trench the second, and the largest holes the third. Builders rotated each successive early mosque to align it with Mecca as the means of determining proper orientation improved. The stone walls belong to two mosques of the 10th and 11th centuries.

muscles by constructing an entire complex of monumental stone buildings surrounded by a stone wall. Like the mosques, these structures rested on the ruins of earlier wooden buildings and may have formed a ceremonial center or a royal compound.

Horton further contends that the Lamu archipelago functioned as a "single commercial and political entity" from the eighth to the 11th century. According to Horton's theory, Manda had been the commercial center, while nearby Shanga, with its stone mosque and administrative buildings, had been the state's ceremonial capital and the site of its royal court.

While some of the questions surrounding Manda's origins and development are now being answered, Kanbalu remains one of East Africa's lost cities. During the latter half of the first millennium, it was the principal point of contact for trade with the Red Sea and the Persian Gulf. But although numerous sites for Kanbalu have been proposed, there is no conclusive archaeological evidence to point to any one spot.

The few available clues are to be found only in historical sources. An eyewitness report by the noted 10th-century Arab geographer al-Masudi describes Kanbalu as a port on an island off the coast of East Africa. He further notes that Kanbalu had been founded around AD 750 and that at the time of his visit in 916 Islam had not yet made serious inroads into the town. Traditionally, Kanbalu has been associated with Pemba, an island off the coast of Tanzania, 225 miles south of the Lamu archipelago. A reference in a 13th-century Arabic geographical dictionary lists Pemba as Jazirat al-Khadra, "Isle of Verdure"—the site of two cities, one of them called Mknblu, the other Mtnby.

In 1953 the British archaeologist James Kirkman noted the linguistic similarity between Mknblu and Ras Mkumbuu, a site on Pemba where stone ruins exist. He conducted a series of excavations there, in the hope the site might yield evidence of the fabled Kanbalu of the 10th century. To his disappointment, he was unable to uncover any signs of habitation before the 13th century. In 1984 Mark Horton dug a trench at Ras Mkumbuu but had no more luck than Kirkman in establishing an earlier date for the site. Expanding his search, Horton started digging on Mtambwe Mkuu, an islet just off the western edge of Pemba.

There, in 1985, while excavating the remains of a modest wooden house, Horton made a startling discovery. He came upon the remnants of a decayed cloth bag that had been shut with a silver clasp. Inside were more than 2,000 coins, the latest dating significantly to AD 1066. Ten of the coins were made of gold, the rest silver, and these were inscribed with the names of African rulers. Undoubtedly, the silver coins had been minted locally, and like those of Horton's find at Shanga, they were patterned on coins produced by the Fatimid caliphs of Sicily. Seven of the gold ones proved to be genuine Fatimid dinars from mints in Tunisia, Egypt, Syria, and Tyre, while the remaining three were imitations of unknown origin. The coins may well have been hidden on Mtambwe Mkuu by someone from Pemba, and this helps give credence to the theory that the island indeed holds the long-lost city of Kanbalu, where such a fortune could easily have been amassed by one of the traders dealing with the Arabic world.

A number of the coins in the Mtambwe Mkuu hoard bore the name of Ali bin al-Hasan, a legendary sultan whose exploits are documented in the sometimes fanciful *Kilwa Chronicle*. Based on oral tra-

Gold coins unearthed on the island of Pemba, off Kenya, testify to 11th-century Swahili trade with the Arab world. Six of the above coins are Fatimid dinars from Syrian, Egyptian, Tunisian, and Tyrian mints. The three coins closest to the caption are thought to be copies of the currency, with imitation Arabic script. All of them formed part of a hoard that was buried in AD 1066 and discovered in 1984, which contained more than 2,000 other gold and silver African coins.

ditions not written down until the 16th century, the *Kilwa Chronicle* survives today in two forms: an abridged Portuguese translation that was published in 1552, and a 19th-century copy of the original Arabic account. Although they differ somewhat in detail from each other, both of the versions purport to be the history of Kilwa, a Swahili city that flourished on the island of the same name and had been the most important port in East Africa from the 12th to the 15th century. In fact, it was in this city that the Swahili culture quite literally had enjoyed its golden age. According to the *Kilwa Chronicle,* the city originated in the 10th century when a father and his six sons, each in his own ship, left their native Shiraz in Persia, and one of the sons, the same Ali bin al-Hasan, established a sultanate at Kilwa. Rather than an invasion, the takeover is depicted as a peaceable business transaction in which the would-be sultan obtained Kilwa from "an infidel from Muli" in exchange for a bolt of cloth long enough to encircle the island. Once installed as the lord of his own newly acquired realm, Ali supposedly ruled for 40 years.

Although the *Kilwa Chronicle* often corroborates archaeological findings, it is not only partly mythical but also sometimes erroneous, placing Kilwa's founding in the 10th century, for example, whereas the physical evidence pushes the date back to the ninth or even the eighth century. As for Ali bin al-Hasan's Shiraz roots, Mark Horton raises questions about the *Kilwa Chronicle*'s version, arguing that Ali hailed from the Lamu archipelago, not Shiraz. Other scholars suggest that his claim to such a heritage was more allegorical than literal, that the new sultan and his successors were, in effect, wrapping themselves in the flag of Islam in order to strengthen their own claim to legitimacy.

But if Ali bin al-Hasan's provenance is questionable, his existence is not, as evidenced by the hundreds of recovered coins that bear his name. In fact, excavations at Kilwa itself, begun in 1958 by Neville Chittick, turned up more than 400 copper coins inscribed with the name of Kilwa's founding sultan. Based on the depth of these deposits, Chittick assigned a late 12th-century date to the start of the Shirazi dynasty, some two centuries later than the date suggested by the *Kilwa Chronicle.*

Those same excavations revealed that, prior to the Shirazi period, Kilwa's people lived in wattle-and-daub homes and subsisted

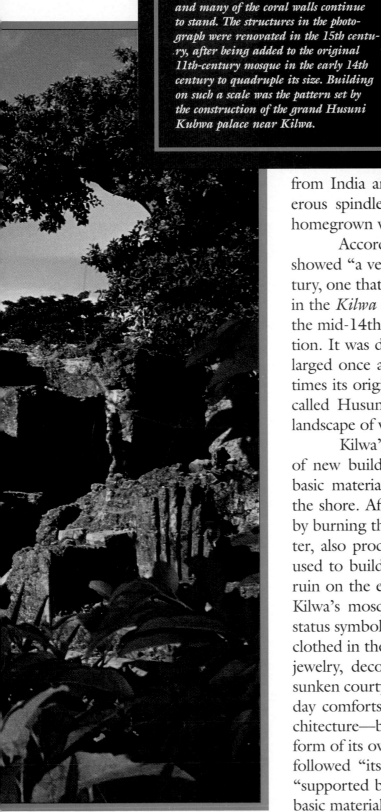

by fishing and gathering shellfish. Imported goods, rare during Kilwa's earliest days, became increasingly more common at levels that coincided with the onset of the Shirazi period. By this time, too, the town's population was at least partly Muslim, as indicated by the discovery of three Muslim burials and a mosque. Imports included large numbers of glass beads from India and a significant amount of Chinese porcelain. Numerous spindle whorls found at these levels hinted at a thriving, homegrown weaving industry.

According to Chittick, the archaeological evidence also showed "a very marked cultural break" at the end of the 13th century, one that seems to coincide with a change of dynasty alluded to in the *Kilwa Chronicle*. In his formal report, Chittick wrote that by the mid-14th century Kilwa had reached its highest level of civilization. It was during this period that the island's Great Mosque, enlarged once already in the 13th century, was rebuilt again to four times its original size. Soon afterward, an enormous clifftop palace called Husuni Kubwa was constructed, its roofline a voluptuous landscape of vaults and domes spanning more than 100 rooms.

Kilwa's affluence could be measured not just in the number of new buildings but in its monumental construction style. The basic material was so-called coral rag, obtained from cliffs along the shore. After being joined together by a cement that was made by burning the coral, the blocks were smoothly covered with a plaster, also produced from the burned coral. (Similar materials were used to build the abandoned city of Gedi in Kenya, the first such ruin on the east coast to be archaeologically investigated.) Around Kilwa's mosque and palace, expansive coral-built houses became status symbols for Kilwa's elite. Within these homes, the aristocracy, clothed in the finest silk and cotton and bedecked in silver and gold jewelry, decorated rooms with Chinese porcelain, entertained in sunken courtyards, tended their gardens, and enjoyed such modern-day comforts as indoor plumbing, including bidets. The city's architecture—both monumental and residential—had evolved into a form of its own, partly African, partly Arabic, and wholly Swahili. It followed "its own course," as archaeologist Peter Garlake put it, "supported by the skills of artisans working and exploiting a single basic material to its limits."

At Kilwa, this new building style was best exemplified by Husuni Kubwa, the largest precolonial building in East Africa. The palace was, in the opinion of Garlake, "the fountainhead of all the post-13th century architecture of the coast." Moreover, it epitomized "the true architectural style of the coast with a variety and splendor never again achieved." Probably built on orders from the sultan al-Hasan ibn Talut, most of the structure consisted of reception rooms and apartments, among them his private quarters, which were linked by corridors and arranged around sunken courtyards and an octagonal pool.

Adjoining the palace section was a huge warehouse wing that was composed of dozens of storerooms enclosing a vast central courtyard. Scholars speculate that the construction of Husuni Kubwa might have represented an attempt on the part of the sultan to tighten control over trade by literally putting it under one roof —his own. Alternatively, the palace's warehouse might have been intended as a custom house to facilitate the levying of taxes on the island's trade. In either case, the effort appears to have failed, since the archaeological evidence suggests that Husuni Kubwa may have been abandoned before it was ever occupied or, for that matter, before it was even completed.

As the boom town of the East African coast in the 14th century, with a population of perhaps 20,000, Kilwa could be counted on to impress its visitors, not the least of whom was the world-traveler Ibn Battuta. Writing some years after his 1331 sojourn in Kilwa, he still remembered the port as "one of the most beautiful and well-constructed towns in the world"—high praise from a man whose 29 years of wandering had by then carried him through dozens of countries on two continents.

But the city's splendor was short-lived: By the end of the 15th century Kilwa found itself weakened at home by political intrigue, diminished abroad by a northward shift in the gold trade, and no longer in control of its own destiny. Its fate, like that of much of East Africa, would soon be in the hands of the Portuguese.

Some 1,200 miles southwest of Kilwa lay Great Zimbabwe, the inland terminus of the gold pipeline to the coast and the hub of a trading network whose spokes radiated across the Zimbabwe Plateau. Great Zimbabwe's history was always closely intertwined with that of its East African trading partners, as evidenced by a hoard of arti-

facts unearthed in one of its stone enclosures in 1903. In addition to ivory, gold, and large quantities of locally made wares, the hoard contained Chinese ceramics, tens of thousands of glass beads from India, and a Persian faience bowl from the 13th or the 14th century.

Almost seven decades later, in 1971, the American archaeologist Thomas Huffman found a single badly worn copper coin in the ruins of Great Zimbabwe. Minted in the 14th century, it bore the name of Sultan al-Hasan bin Sulaiman, the same ruler who had greeted Ibn Battuta on his visit to Kilwa in 1331.

The groundbreaking systematic work by David Randall-MacIver and Gertrude Caton-Thompson had proven that Great Zimbabwe was built by the ancestors of today's Shona people. But subsequent archaeological investigations have too often focused on who built Great Zimbabwe and when, while ignoring the even more important questions of why Great Zimbabwe was settled and exactly how it rose to prominence.

Husuni Kubwa palace sprawls on Kilwa Island, off the Tanzanian coast, in this reconstruction based on the work of British archaeologist Peter Garlake. Ruins now mark the site from which sultans ruled Kilwa during the 1300s and oversaw its gold trade, profits from which helped finance the building of the palace. Constructed largely from local coral rag, the palace featured a large warehouse courtyard with a quarry pit (top), as well as smaller courtyards and a pool (center).

Any understanding of the origins of Great Zimbabwe must begin with the environmental and cultural influences that nurtured its growth. Geographically, the Zimbabwe Plateau is framed north and south by the valleys of the Zambezi and Limpopo Rivers, respectively. To the east lies the wide coastal plain that abuts the Indian Ocean, while to the west the rolling woodlands and savanna gradually give way to the inhospitable Kalahari Desert.

A combination of factors made this high plateau especially suitable for human habitation, including ample rainfall, extensive grazing land, fertile soil, and readily available timber. Most important, the plateau was generally free of the dreaded tsetse fly and the sleeping sickness that the insect brought to cattle and people. Not far away, too, were the gold fields—as well as sources of copper, iron, and tin—that would play so important a role in the history of Great Zimbabwe.

During the first millennium AD, the Zimbabwe Plateau's benign climate spawned a culture and economy based on cattle herding and farming. The long-horn breed indigenous to that area became the measure of an individual's wealth, more stable than currency and more practical than gold. But the demand first for ivory and then for gold by the coastal Swahili, for their trading partners in the Arabic and Mediterranean worlds, spurred the development of trade. Although such commodities had little intrinsic value to the Shona, they could be exchanged for beads, fine cloth, and other coveted foreign goods.

In time, profits generated by trade created a surplus of wealth—both in livestock and imported goods—concentrated in the hands of a few people, who emerged as a ruling elite. At such early second-millennium sites as Mapungubwe, the stratification of society was clearly evident in a settlement pattern that saw the rulers appropriately situated high on the hilltop, while the lower classes set up housekeeping down the slope.

Wealth in such settlements tended to flow upward, as the leaders profited from both trade and tribute. Not much trickled down to the peasants, and the little that did came in return for their hard labor. As the rich grew richer, they increasingly saw themselves as separate and above the rest. Eventually, stone walls were built to enclose the hilltop enclaves of the nobility—walls that were, in Peter Garlake's words, "essentially a political statement."

Hundreds of such enclosures once dotted the Zimbabwe Plateau. The ruins of at least 150 survive today, but as many as 50 more have been completely destroyed since the beginning of the 20th century. Largest of all was Great Zimbabwe, which prospered on the gold trade from about AD 1250 to 1450 and emerged as the cultural and political capital of the Zimbabwe state.

Great Zimbabwe consists of three main parts, which are spread over about 100 acres: the Hill Ruin, a cluster of stone enclosures built atop a granite cliff; the so-called Great Enclosure, probably a royal court or ritual center surrounded by about a dozen similarly shaped but smaller enclosures; and a perimeter town where the majority of the population lived. Radiocarbon dating indicates that although the site may have been temporarily occupied as early as the fourth century AD, the first permanent settlement was not established there until the 10th, or perhaps even the 11th, century. By the 12th century Great Zimbabwe, with its cattle wealth and its proximity to the gold fields as leverage, was already moving toward domination of regional trade.

Early estimates of the city's population ranged from only

1,000 to 2,500 adults, perhaps 100 or 200 of whom composed Great Zimbabwe's ruling elite. But newer figures, based on research commencing in the early 1970s by Thomas Huffman, suggest that as many as 18,000 people may have called Great Zimbabwe home. This upward revision seems more credible: As the cultural center of the state and the focus of its wealth, Great Zimbabwe would have acted as an urban magnet, attracting the ambitious and the hopeful from outlying areas.

As with other cases of rural exodus throughout history, most of those fleeing the countryside in search of a better life found a quite different reality, living under conditions comparable to modern tenements and slums. A leading historian of Zimbabwe, David N. Beach, has vividly evoked the scene: "This was urban living," writes Beach. "Inside the wall that enclosed the main site, the huts were so close together that their eaves must have been nearly touching. A

Part of the most excavated site in East Africa, the Great Mosque at Gedi on the Kenyan coast still retains its outline. An outer wall of the main prayer hall stands behind the fallen ruins of the ablution area, where worshipers would cleanse themselves with water from the well in the foreground before entering the mosque. The latest of three mosques at the site, this one dates to the mid-16th century.

great deal of the valley, now green, must have been trampled bare by the passage of feet. From cockcrow to evening, the noise must have been tremendous. In certain weather conditions the smoke from hundreds if not thousands of cooking fires would have created conditions approaching that of smog."

Beach further notes that poor sanitary conditions would have certainly bred disease and could hardly have enhanced the mystique long associated with the site. "Zimbabwe has often been viewed through an aura of romance," he concludes, "but perhaps a cloud of smoke and flies would be more appropriate from a standpoint of archaeological accuracy. The contrast between the rulers and the ruled must have been quite striking."

Nowhere was that contrast more apparent than inside the magnificent stone walls that form Great Zimbabwe's various enclosures. Even in their present ruined state, they offer a haunting glimpse of what life was like for the ruler and his relatives as well as for the priests and the bureaucrats who composed Great Zimbabwe's governing elite. Excavations have revealed that the walls are, in fact, all that remain of what Peter Garlake has called, "an architecture that is unparalleled elsewhere in Africa or beyond."

In their earliest incarnation, the enclosures held only a few circular dwellings made of *daga,* a cementlike mud whose ingredients included the clay found locally in termite mounds. But as Great Zimbabwe grew in importance, new walls were built to enclose more space. Within these compounds, shorter lengths of wall functioned as both structural support for additional daga houses and privacy screens between neighbors and their adjacent courtyards.

Almost one million granite blocks went into the construction of the 800-foot-long outer wall around the Great Enclosure. The prodigious human effort needed to move, cut, dress, and position all of those blocks was eased somewhat by a combination of geology and climate. Granite was plentiful on the Zimbabwe Plateau, where, thanks to the wide fluctuation in temperature between the hot days and the chilly nights, the rock naturally split into parallel-sided slabs that peeled away from the hillsides. This natural, so-called onion-skin exfoliation could be accelerated by hammering wedges into cracks or by building a fire atop a dome of rock, then dousing it quickly with cold water.

Whether split by nature or human hands, the granite building blocks were of such regular shape that they could be stacked without mortar. The walls built from these blocks were typically about twice as high as they were thick—anywhere from 4 to 17 feet—and wriggled across the landscape in seeming disregard for the terrain. There were no straight sections and no sharp angles, only curves, and the evidence indicates that the walls never supported roofs. Some featured herringbone, dentil, or chevron patterns created by incorporating lines of sloping blocks into the stonework. The walls of Great Zimbabwe apparently had no defensive purpose, but they did raise masonry to an art form, as the original stonework was progressively embellished with rounded gateways, timber-linteled doors, stepped platforms, turrets, towers, and flights of stairs sculpted into elegant curves.

In fact, variations in the quality of the stonework have helped experts to date the occupation periods of Great Zimbabwe's enclosures. Based on fieldwork that was conducted in 1958, the British archaeologists Roger Summers and Keith Robinson and the architect Anthony Whitty managed to identify several distinct styles of masonry. According to the most recent thinking, the earliest phase probably dates to the 13th century and features undressed stones—irregular in size and shape—laid without a foundation in uneven courses. In the mid-14th century Great Zimbabwe's masons displayed the greatest mastery of their art; the blocks were carefully matched, expertly dressed, and laid in long, level courses, which sometimes bottomed out in a shallow foundation trench. In contrast, the newest walls, dating from the 15th century, betray an unmistakable—and enigmatic—decline in skills. The stones are haphazardly laid, roughly piled, and wedged together.

There are no written accounts of any European ever visiting Great Zimbabwe in its prime, nor are there any surviving Arab descriptions. Archaeological evidence does point to the presence of Swahili traders in Great Zimbabwe, but although the Swahili were literate, they failed to leave a record that perhaps would have shed some light on the origins of the settlement. Some European chroniclers who visited Africa seasoned their books with hearsay about places they had not seen.

The Portuguese historian João de Barros, for example, repeated what he had been told about a grand ruin near the gold fields, "a square fortress, of masonry within and without, built of stones of marvelous size, and there appears to be no mortar joining them." But de Barros was writing in 1552, when Great Zimbabwe had already slipped into obscurity, and although he did call such edifices Symbaoe, it is likely that he was describing one of Great Zimbabwe's successor capitals, possibly Khami.

Of course, it was precisely the proximity of these Symbaoe to the gold fields that interested the Portuguese in the first place. But while wealth to a European was best tallied in ounces of gold, even at its peak Great Zimbabwe remained a cattle-herding culture and counted its prosperity on the heads of its livestock.

Still, trade had given Great Zimbabwe an opportunity to diversify its economy, providing the city with some insurance against what the Shona called *shangwa*, a drought or other natural disaster that could destroy their way of life. Trade had also made Great Zimbabwe the regional entrepôt for a flood of raw materials from distant areas of the Zimbabwe state.

As a result, the city became the focal point for the development of crafts. Iron was smelted and forged into tools and weapons. Copper, bronze, and gold were also worked here and fashioned into jewelry or hammered into sheathing used to envelop wooden carvings. In addition, large quantities of spindle whorls indicate that spinning and weaving played a significant role in life at Great Zimbabwe. Pottery was also manufactured, and soapstone was carved into dishes, figurines, and casting molds, as well as ritual figures and monoliths. Although some of this merchandise may have traveled far afield in trade, most of Great Zimbabwe's gross national product stayed closer to home and was exchanged for goods produced by neighboring cultures.

Great Zimbabwe was only the largest and the most powerful of a whole hierarchy of similar sites scattered across the plateau, many of which functioned as provincial courts. Some, such as Chumnungwa, rivaled the size and sophistication of Great Zimbabwe itself. Others, including Ruanga, were much smaller and could accommodate no more than 10 adults. These were almost certainly the residences of governors appointed by the Zimbabwe state to oversee the collection of tribute, mostly gold.

Unfortunately, many such sites were ransacked by European treasure hunters during the late 19th century, and few have ever undergone more than a cursory archaeological survey. Indeed, most of the scientific effort devoted to the investigation of the Zimbabwe

GREAT ZIMBABWE: STONE STRUCTURES THAT SPEAK OF POWER AND GRANDEUR

Once it was a thriving capital grown rich on the gold trade. Today Great Zimbabwe recalls its vanished glory in a scattering of curving, granite walls spread over some 100 hilly acres. Dominating the site is the Great Enclosure *(below)*, an oval space surrounded by a wall more than 800 feet long, as much as 17 feet thick, and 32 feet high.

The purpose of the Great Enclosure puzzles scholars. It may have been the abode of the king's first or senior wife or as one archaeologist proposes, basing his idea on recent ethnographic practices, a school to tutor adolescents in morals, sex, and etiquette before marriage. Built between the 12th and the 15th century AD by ancestors of the present Shona people, the Great Enclosure and other structures nearby rose taking advantage of a natural phenomenon—the cleavage of local granite by fluctuations between hot daytime and cold nighttime temperatures. Breaking off in slabs, the stone made a ready construction material. Masons dressed the pieces into smaller, matching-size blocks with fist-size, round hammerstones of hard dolerite, then built them up in two parallel rows, filling the space between with rubble. Part of the structures may have been plastered with *daga,* a wet mixture of decomposed granite and gravel still used for houses.

On an outcrop above the valley is the Hill Ruin, a maze of walls where the kings probably lived and held court. At the structure's eastern end various relics have been found—among them carved soapstone birds, considered symbolic messengers between the living and the spirits of departed rulers. Such finds suggest this sector was a center of political and religious activity for the Zimbabwe state.

In this panorama, the Great Enclosure looms above 12 circular compounds where the elite are believed to have dwelled in round houses, now reduced to mounds of clay and gravel. These dwellings were connected by walls to form individual family compounds. Outside this special area thousands of common people lived in daga huts, densely clustered throughout the valley.

The outer wall of the Great Enclosure (above) slopes gently inward for stability, each course set back slightly from the one below. Decorating the top of this southeastern portion is a double chevron pattern, a common African motif. Running between the outer and the inner wall is a walkway known as the Parallel Passage (below). Because the outer wall was erected last, it displays the fully developed stone technique of the Zimbabwe masons. Entry steps (left) flow directly from the wall, looping into ever sharper arcs as they climb.

Rising within the Great Enclosure, a cone-shaped structure gives the elliptical compound a spectacular visual focus. Dubbed the Conical Tower, it is a solid mass, about 30 feet high and 18 feet in diameter. Archaeologists speculate that it may represent a grain silo, a metaphor for male power, while the round structure in front may have been an emblem of the status of Great Zimbabwe's senior women.

state has been expended at Great Zimbabwe alone. And even there, most excavations have taken place within the enclosures themselves, despite the fact that the vast majority of the citizens lived outside the walls. In effect, scholars have focused 90 percent of their studies on just two percent of the population.

Now archaeologists are attempting to redress this imbalance by broadening the investigation at Great Zimbabwe and by focusing on the Zimbabwe state as a whole. As a result, a more complete picture of daily life is emerging, revealing, for example, that while the ruling elite may have lived in relative splendor at Great Zimbabwe, most peasants resided not in or around such enclosures but in small unwalled villages.

While there may have been hundreds of such settlements dating from the height of Zimbabwe's power, only a few have ever been identified or excavated, among them Chivowa Hill and Montevideo Ranch. Beginning in 1976 both of these were studied by the archaeologist Paul Sinclair of Sweden's Uppsala University, who noted, not surprisingly, that life here revolved around the herding of cattle. But Sinclair also found evidence of iron smelting and spinning, and he speculated that the residents may have done a little gold prospecting on the side.

Gold mining was, in fact, the lot of the peasant class throughout the Zimbabwe state, and it was usually done during the agricultural off-season, either by panning, digging open pits, or if absolutely necessary, sinking shafts into deeper deposits. The work could be downright dangerous, as evidenced by the number of skeletons discovered in abandoned shafts. And for all of their labor, the peasants gained little; the ruling class had claim to any recovered gold. Much of what is known about gold extraction and production in the area comes from the extensive and thorough investigations conducted by Roger Summers.

It was gold that, inevitably, brought the Portuguese to the shores of East Africa and eventually to the interior in search of the mines. The temptation of what the famed explorer Vasco da Gama himself called *infinito ouro*—infinite gold—led to bloody conflicts that would disrupt long-established patterns of commerce and bring down whole societies.

By then, however, Great Zimbabwe's dominance of the region and its trade was already history. Numerous reasons have been

A lone monolith looks east over the Zimbabwe Plateau from its perch atop a wall of the Hill Ruin at Great Zimbabwe. Dozens of such monoliths once adorned the walls of the structure, but archaeologists are unsure why. Theories abound: The monoliths may have represented ancestral lineage or been symbols of power or served as monuments to the history of the state.

proposed for the decline, but none has been—or indeed can be—definitively proven. Since the inhabitants left no written records, scholars can only offer educated speculation based on physical evidence. It is possible that Great Zimbabwe's large population may have brought about its own shangwa by imposing too great a demand on the environment (depleting stores of firewood, for example, or exhausting the fertility of the soil). Whatever the causes, the ultimate effect was the dispersal of the city's population, some of whom subsequently established a new Shona state, Torwa, with its own stone-walled capital at Khami.

Change was also the order of the day along the East African coast at the start of the 16th century, where relations between the Swahili and the newly arrived Portuguese had gotten off to a bumpy start. The Swahili rightly viewed these newcomers as a threat to the Swahili monopoly on the gold trade with the interior. Things grew even worse after the Portuguese sacked Kilwa in 1505. In the end, the Portuguese succeeded only in disrupting longstanding trade routes, severing vital links between the coast and the gold fields, and ruining an economy and a way of life that had thrived for centuries. For Kilwa and for Great Zimbabwe's successor states in the interior, the outcome was catastrophic. As Peter Garlake has observed, "The civilizations of the coast and the southern plateau were almost entirely extinguished."

Afterward, silence slowly settled over the dozens of abandoned Swahili settlements up and down the coast, as it had even earlier over the ruins of Great Zimbabwe. And yet those sites have always spoken to those who would dare to listen: pioneering archaeologists such as David Randall-MacIver, Neville Chittick, and Gertrude Caton-Thompson, and a new generation that includes Mark Horton and Peter Garlake.

These scholars and others have finally laid to rest the Eurocentric bias of the colonial period, which had for so long insisted that Africans were incapable of creating anything as urbane and distinctive as the palace and Great Mosque at Kilwa or the walls of Great Zimbabwe. Kilwa, so this reasoning went, must have been built by Arabs and the ruins of the interior must belong to a mysterious, long-vanished, non-African race. Nonsense, said Caton-Thompson as far back as 1931, when she wrote that the only mystery about Zimbabwe "is the mystery which lies in the still pulsating heart of native Africa."

AFRICA'S ENDURING HERITAGE

Among Africa's greatest resources are the diversity and resilience of its people. More than a thousand distinct ethnic groups speaking 800 languages occupy the broad swath of land south of the Sahara. Since before the dawn of written history, these disparate groups have spawned a wide variety of cultures and societies and followed many different paths to greatness.

Bounded on all sides by ocean and desert, the inhabitants of sub-Saharan Africa long welcomed contact with other parts of the world and showed a receptiveness to numerous imported ideas—but without sacrificing their identity in the process. Even the ancient Nubians along the Upper Nile, who were influenced culturally and politically by Egypt during the time of the pharaohs, never lost sight of their own traditions. Similarly, many later Africans, in both the east and the west, embraced Islam and incorporated facets of Arab culture into their own while forging vast kingdoms

and empires that remained wholly African in character.

Few of these great medieval African states survived intact the 19th-century partition of the continent by the European colonial powers, who almost entirely destroyed Africa's political and economic independence. But, fortunately, the modern world's knowledge of what life was like in precolonial days is not restricted to the testimony of excavation pits or artifacts, however striking. For although African regimes succumbed to Europe's colonialism, African culture persevered in countless ways, and many long-lived traditions still survive.

The relatively new discipline of ethnoarchaeology examines the customs, art, and architecture of the present to open wider the window on the past provided by archaeology. For example, the floor plan and construction methods used by the Shona in the modern *imba* (*above*) have remained unchanged since at least the 1300s, when Great Zimbabwe was at its height.

Dancing and wrestling are leit-motifs bridging millennia of African culture. Even today, wrestling remains a popular contest of personal strength and finesse from Senegal to the Sudan, and almost every village festival or special ceremony involves traditional dancing.

Researchers study these venerable customs in order to gain some insight into a society's history where no written records or tangible artifacts from the distant past exist. But while an examination of a group's contemporary rituals sometimes reveals tantalizing links between ancient and modern Africa, it by no means offers investigators conclusive data.

As Adria LaViolette, an archaeologist at the University of Virginia, states, "Any masked dance performed today is a new interpretation of the dance—it changes subtly in meaning every time it's done." Furthermore, no part of late 20th-century Africa, however isolated it may appear to be, is untouched by the outside world.

One dance performed by the cliff-dwelling Dogon of northeastern Mali, for example, includes a masked figure of a "European doctor" who moves among the crowd pretending to examine patients. Even so, the intrinsic forms of rituals like this—and the cultural impetus behind them—survive.

A wall relief from the funerary temple of Ramses III depicts Nubians wrestling for the pharaoh's enjoyment. The present-day Nuba of southern Sudan employ a similar style in their matches (left). But archaeologists hesitate to rely solely on comparisons of wrestling technique to verify an ethnic link between two cultures separated by 3,000 years.

This 19th-century Dogon statue portrays two musicians playing a balafon—a melodious instrument consisting of wooden keys laid over hollow wooden resonators. No one knows when or where it originated, since wooden artifacts rarely survive the ravages of a tropical climate for more than a couple of centuries. Dogon dance, however, like the evocative Dama ceremony (above)—which facilitates passage to the afterlife—has persevered (albeit with modifications) as it has been passed down from one generation to the next.

In the art of traditional African societies, form closely follows function. There is very little art for art's sake; every piece must have a purpose and fulfill a need. Examples of items lavished with artistic devotion run from the prosaic (ceramic storage containers, baskets, utensils, furniture, musical instruments, blankets, and articles of clothing) to the consequential (key buildings, religious icons, and personal markers of cultural identity and social rank).

In a broad range of mediums —including the human body— African artists have always produced works of brilliance. But, in the past, Western art connoisseurs tended to regard such endeavors as crafts rather than true art. This specious, culturally biased presumption has been laid to rest, and the world at large has come to appreciate the breadth, the ingenuity, and the inherent flair of African art. Indeed, since the 1960s, the art history departments of most major universities have added courses on African art to their curricula.

Meanwhile, ethnoarchaeologists and art historians strive to comprehend the creative stimulus behind the art—its purpose within the culture—so that each piece may be understood in its own context.

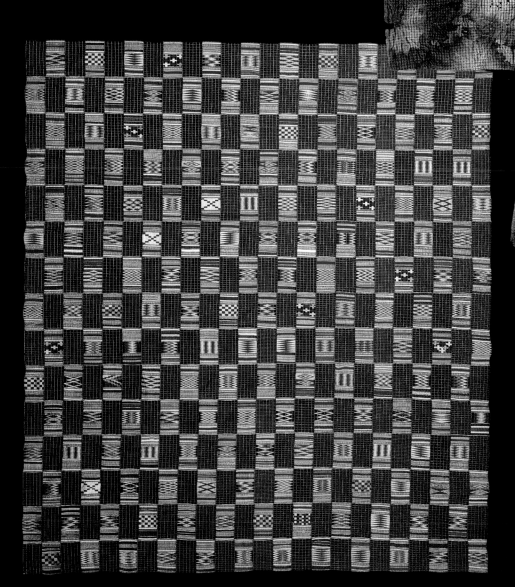

Vibrant colors, intricate designs, and a tight weave are the hallmarks of kente cloth (left). This contemporary example—a man's wrap called a kubi —is from Bonwire, Ghana, ancient center of weaving. In the same manner as the exceedingly rare fragment of 800-year-old fabric shown above, modern kente cloth is woven in long, narrow strips that are stitched together to form the finished piece.

Facial scarification is an age-old badge of adulthood and ethnic affiliation in Africa. Patterns may have changed since the 12th century, when an artist at Jenné-jeno sculpted this terra-cotta head, but the tradition survives, as evidenced by the modern West African woman (above, right). Soot is often rubbed into the cuts to give them a darkened and raised appearance when they heal.

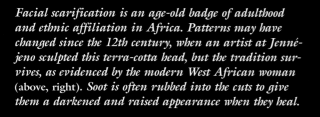

Beads constitute one of the oldest and most popular forms of African adornment. These four strands unearthed in Nubia are more than 2,000 years old. The manner in which beads are worn carries social significance within many African cultures. This young woman of the nomadic Wodaabe people is attired for the Geerewol ceremony. Her trappings indicate she has come in search of a husband.

Absorbed in his half-formed soapstone
figure, the Shona sculptor Crispin June
Mutambika upholds the artistic legacy
of his forebears. Art experts note a con-
sistency not just of medium and technique
but of style between modern works such
as Mutambika's and these two soapstone
birds, among the few masterpieces not pil-
fered from the ruins of Great Zimbabwe
by late 19th-century treasure hunters.
One French art critic wrote, "The Shona
sculptors appeared to pick up their tools
where their ancestors of several hundred
years before had laid them down."

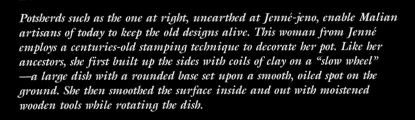

Potsherds such as the one at right, unearthed at Jenné-jeno, enable Malian artisans of today to keep the old designs alive. This woman from Jenné employs a centuries-old stamping technique to decorate her pot. Like her ancestors, she first built up the sides with coils of clay on a "slow wheel"—a large dish with a rounded base set upon a smooth, oiled spot on the ground. She then smoothed the surface inside and out with moistened wooden tools while rotating the dish.

AESTHETIC AND PRACTICAL DESIGNS

The sweeping diversity of climate and terrain across sub-Saharan Africa has generated a myriad of architectural styles and construction techniques. Of necessity, peoples all over the continent have used materials at hand to build the visible manifestations of their society. By studying these structures, researchers can glean valuable cultural data—from the size and makeup of the basic family unit to the priority and organization of daily activities, and even how much the culture values privacy.

The Nubians quarried blocks of granite and sandstone from the bluffs along the upper Nile to construct magnificent temples, palaces, and pyramids. The Swahili mined coastal deposits of hardened, fossilized coral to build their port cities. And at Great Zimbabwe, masons took advantage of the local granite, shaped by nature into conveniently sized chunks that could be put up without mortar. In the absence of these more durable building materials, some African cultures have created massive, multistoried architectural wonders out of nothing more than sun-dried mud bricks and a few pieces of wood. The use of local materials enables each of these diverse styles to blend harmoniously into its particular setting.

Lamu Island (off the Kenyan coast), site of the 150-year old mosque above, remains a strong center of Swahili culture. Still serving the current population, the building exhibits a distinctive style and coral construction that reflect centuries-old Swahili conventions. A Dogon village (right) perches on a steep slope in Mali. Isolated in their cliff-face aeries, the Dogon build their stone and mud houses in the same manner their

Exposed wooden supports—called toron—
reveal the continuity of architectural style
between the early 14th-century Sankore
Mosque (above) at Timbuktu and the
Great Mosque at Jenné (right), completed
in 1907. Each year at the end of the rainy
season, the mud-plastered facade must be
repaired and smoothed by hand. Elegant
and immense, these majestic structures
commemorate the Niger River region's
long affiliation with Islam, yet their architecture remains uniquely African.

A GRAND TAPESTRY OF VIVID CULTURES

Africa, the world's second largest continent, is a land of extremes. To the north and the south lie the scorching Sahara and Kalahari Deserts. In between are the luxuriant rain forests of the Congo basin and the Gulf of Guinea coast; lofty, snow-crested volcanoes; endless savanna; and the Great Rift Valley. Parts of Africa's interior situated well above sea level enjoy a pleasant climate despite their tropical latitudes, but vast areas lying at lower elevations suffer from debilitating heat and unreliable precipitation. Furthermore, all of the scourges that are endemic to the tropics, afflicting humans, animals, and crops, are to be found here.

Nevertheless, it was Africa that served as the cradle of the human race. Fossil records show that *Homo erectus,* the tool-wielding primate that would evolve into *Homo sapiens,* appeared on the grassy highlands of East Africa more than a million years ago.

Several of Africa's first sedentary agricultural societies emerged more than 8,000 years ago in what would later become the world's largest desert. The Sahara at that time, though, was a far different place, as shown by surviving rock paintings and engravings. Here cycles of abundant rainfall produced vegetation that attracted herds of game; these in turn drew nomadic hunter-gatherers, who in time settled down as farmers and herders.

But around the fourth millennium BC the climate began to change, and the lakes and rivers slowly dried up. Over time, the Sahara became a forbidding impediment to both travel and habitation. And yet, in one area, where the waters of the Nile created a narrow, green ribbon of life from the parched desert, some of Africa's first advanced societies would emerge.

Humanity found not only a birthplace in Africa but also a land where, despite nature's harsh conditions, human culture could flourish.

NUBIA 3900 BC–AD 1500

KING OF KUSH

Nubia's history, like neighboring Egypt's, is inexorably linked with the Nile. Along the river's fertile banks, settlements flourished for thousands of years. Lower Nubia's first two major cultures, the so-called A- and C-groups, hunted and fished, farmed and herded in the Nile Valley for more than 2,000 years. Archaeologists exploring the desert cemeteries of these early inhabitants have unearthed large quantities of Egyptian goods, which most likely had been obtained through the exchange of exotic commodities, such as animal skins, rare woods, and ivory from Africa's interior. Still farther south, in Upper Nubia, a group called the Kerma culture, named for its capital city, built large temple complexes and enormous tumulus tombs, which were filled with a wealth of grave goods and a great many human sacrifices. Kerma's nascent monumental architecture and some of its burial practices prefigured a golden age for the land that the Egyptians called Kush.

Kush's monarchy, based alternately in the cities of Napata and Meroë, gradually became strong enough to gain control of Egypt, ruling 60 years as its 25th Dynasty. After losing Egypt to Assyrian invaders, the Kushite kings continued to reign in their increasingly prosperous southern domain. By 300 BC, while Napata remained an important cult center, Meroë became the primary capital, a place where industry, trade, and art and architecture all flourished. Nubia continued to maintain a strong military posture, and Meroitic kings and queens were both portrayed smiting their enemies. The gilded bronze statue of a Kushite ruler *(above)* includes a stone thumb ring used by archers to protect their hands while drawing a bow tight. The Meroitic empire collapsed in the mid-fourth century AD, although vestiges of the culture remained until AD 550, most notably in the cities of Ballana and Qustul.

Converted to Christianity by Byzantine missionaries at the end of the sixth century, a host of smaller Nubian kingdoms rose and fell until all eventually were subsumed into Africa's Arab and Islamic world in the early 16th century.

WEST AFRICA
1500 BC-AD 1500

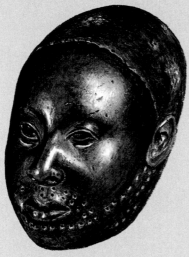

IFE COPPER MASK

THE EAST COAST AND ZIMBABWE
AD 100-1500

SWAHILI COIN

West Africa, home to great African empires and kingdoms, is bounded to the north by the Sahara and to the south by the equatorial waters of the Gulf of Guinea. In between lie three distinct ecological zones: the dry, dusty Sahel; the broad savanna and woodlands; and the tropical rain forest of the coast. The climate and topography of these zones helped to shape the cultures that arose within them, and trade became a common thread, binding them together.

As early as 1000 BC the inhabitants of the Sahel region were living in settled agricultural communities surrounded by high walls and protected with fortified gates. Farther south, where savanna takes over, hundreds of richly appointed burial mounds, dating from as early as the sixth century AD, dot the landscapes of Senegal and Mali. The variety and value of grave goods discovered in these point to the existence of local chieftains who had grown rich on regional trade. As wealth—and eventually political power—became centered in the hands of a ruling elite, socially stratified city-states sprang up throughout the area.

In the savanna, these city-states fought for control of resources and local trade routes and, in time, for the trans-Saharan routes as well. The stronger expanded their influence and boundaries, absorbing the weaker. Large trading empires emerged—first Ghana, then Mali, and finally Songhay. Increasingly Islamic in character after about 1000 AD, these empires were dazzling in their splendor and cosmopolitan in their outlook, the equal of many European states of the day.

South of the savanna, the thick vegetation made far-reaching political control impractical. Here kingdoms and city-states—among them, Benin and Ife—remained small in comparison but were just as opulent as their northern counterparts. Their artists produced some of the finest masterpieces Africa has ever seen, including the approximately 500-year-old Ife copper mask above.

The low-lying islands and palm-fringed shores of the East African coast spawned a unique culture of maritime traders, the Swahili. Excellent sailors, they were also highly proficient businessmen. By the ninth century AD they had integrated their ports into a truly international trade network that brought goods to their merchants from Arabia, India, and even China in exchange for a variety of African items from ivory to gold.

In addition, the Swahili demonstrated a receptiveness to certain foreign ideas. From Arabia, they gained a written language—as evidenced by the locally minted coin above bearing a Swahili ruler's name written in Arabic script—and a religion. By the 12th century most of society was converted to Islam and virtually every coastal city contained mosques built of coral in a distinctive Swahili style. But the Swahili also turned their attention in the other direction—to trade with the African interior.

Roughly 200 miles inland from the coast, the Zimbabwe Plateau, with its favorable climate and extensive grazing land, gave rise to a cattle-based economy and culture. More important to the future of the area, productive gold fields lay close at hand and spurred the interest of the coastal Swahili. A mutually beneficial barter system evolved before long, because, although the precious metal had little intrinsic value to the cattle herders, it could be exchanged for a variety of useful imported goods.

The huge profits generated by this trade created a new social class of extremely wealthy individuals. They constructed hilltop enclosures, called *zimbabwes,* and lived separately and regally within the walls. The most spectacular of these, Great Zimbabwe, is an architectural marvel and a fitting testament to the bygone era of the African gold trade. That trade, along with the fortunes of both the Swahili and the rulers of the Zimbabwe Plateau, declined precipitously after the arrival of the Portuguese in the 16th century.

ACKNOWLEDGMENTS

The editors wish to thank the following individuals and institutions for their valuable assistance:

Michel Chauvet, Nantes, France; Nicholas David, University of Calgary, Calgary, Alberta, Canada; Jeff Fleisher, Williamsburg, Virginia; Mimi Games, Smithsonian Institution, Washington, D.C.; Brigitte Gratien, Institut de Papyrologie et d'Egyptologie, Université de Lille III, Lille, France; James Harris, Ann Arbor, Michigan; Mark Horton, University of Bristol, Bristol, England; Nasri Iskandar, Egyptian Museum, Cairo; Heidrun Klein, Bildarchiv Preussischer Kulturbesitz, Berlin; Marcel Kurz, Paris; John Larson, Oriental Institute Museum, Chicago; Stephan Molitor, Hauptstaatsarchiv, Stuttgart; Francine Ndiaye, Musée de l'Homme, Paris; Stacie Olson, University of Pennsylvania, Philadelphia; Jean-Louis Paudrat, Vaires, France; David W. Phillipson, Cambridge, England; Christopher Roy, University of Iowa Museum of Art, Iowa City; Mohammed Saleh, Egyptian Museum, Cairo; Lisa Snider, Oriental Institute Museum, Chicago; Amy J. Stamples, Smithsonian Institution, Washington, D.C.; John H. Taylor, London; Hope Tinney, Ukama Press, Santa Rosa, California; Kent Weeks, American University, Cairo; Thomas H. Wilson, Southwest Museum, Los Angeles.

PICTURE CREDITS

The sources for the illustrations that appear in this volume are listed below. Credits from left to right are separated by semicolons; credits from top to bottom are separated by dashes.

Cover: The Metropolitan Museum of Art, Gift of Mr. and Mrs. Klaus G. Perls, 1991 (1991.17.49). Background courtesy The Oriental Institute of The University of Chicago. End paper: art by Paul Breeden. 6: Egyptian Museum, Cairo/photo courtesy The Brooklyn Museum. 8: Hauptstaatsarchiv, Stuttgart, Germany. 9: Bildarchiv Preussischer Kulturbesitz, Berlin. 10: National Archives of Zimbabwe. 11: From *Proceedings of the British Academy,* Vol. LXXI (1985). 13: National Archives of Zimbabwe. 14, 15: Pierre Colombel, Paris. 19: Map by Dale Glasgow. 20, 21: Courtesy Museum of Fine Arts, Boston. 22: © British Museum, London. 24: Egyptian Museum, Cairo/foto: Jürgen Liepe. 25: Illustration by Walter B. Emery, from *Egypt in Nubia,* Hutchinson of London/Random House U.K., Ltd., 1965. 26: Daniel Berti, inset © Timothy Kendall. 28: Charles Bonnet. 29: Charles Bonnet—Musée d'Art et d'Histoire, Geneva, photo Jean-Marc Yersin. 30: Daniel Berti—Director's Contingent Fund, courtesy Museum of Fine Arts, Boston. 32-39: Courtesy The Oriental Institute of The University of Chicago. 40: © 1994 Enrico Ferorelli. 42: Courtesy of The Fine Art Society, London. 44: © 1994 Enrico Ferorelli. 45: From *Denkmaeler aus Aegypten und Aethiopien,* by Richard Lepsius, part 5, plate 60, 1842-1845. 46: © 1994 Enrico Ferorelli. 47: Museum Expedition, courtesy Museum of Fine Arts, Boston. 48, 49: Egyptian Expedition of the Metropolitan Museum of Art, Rogers Fund, 1930, 30.4.21. 50, 51: Drawing by Timothy Kendall/courtesy Museum of Fine Arts, Boston-Boston Expedition. 52, 53: Courtesy Egyptian Museum, Cairo; Gift of Theodore Davis, courtesy Museum of Fine Arts, Boston—Egyptian Museum, Cairo/foto: Jürgen Liepe—courtesy Egyptian Museum, Cairo (2). 55: Courtesy Museum of Fine Arts, Boston—Museum Expedition, courtesy Museum of Fine Arts, Boston. 57: © 1994 Enrico Ferorelli. 58: Museum Expedition, courtesy Museum of Fine Arts, Boston—© British Museum, London. 59: © School of Archaeology, Classics and Oriental Studies, University of Liverpool. 60: Staatliche Museen zu Berlin-Preussischer Kulturbesitz, Ägyptisches Museum und Papyrussammlung, foto: Jürgen Liepe. 63: Staatliche Museen zu Berlin-Preussischer Kulturbesitz, Ägyptisches Museum und Papyrussammlung, foto: Margarete Büsing. 64: F. Jackson/Robert Harding Library, London. 65: From *Denkmaeler aus Aegypten und Aethiopien,* by Richard Lepsius, part 5, plate 56, 1842-1845. 66: National Museum, Warsaw—Georg Gerster. 67: National Museum, Warsaw. 68, 69: Egyptian Museum, Cairo/photo courtesy The Brooklyn Museum—Illustrated London News Picture Agency. 71: © 1994 Enrico Ferorelli. 72, 73: © 1994 Enrico Ferorelli (3); drawing © 1990 William Riseman Associates/courtesy Museum of Fine Arts, Boston-Boston Expedition. 74: © 1994 Enrico Ferorelli. 75: © 1994 Enrico Ferorelli—drawing © 1990 William Riseman Associates/courtesy Museum of Fine Arts, Boston-Boston Expedition. 76: © 1994 Enrico Ferorelli; © Timothy Kendall. 77: © 1994 Enrico Ferorelli; drawing by Timothy Kendall. 78, 79: © 1993 William Riseman Associates; © 1994 Enrico Ferorelli. 80: Lee Boltin. 82, 83: M. & A. Kirtley/A.N.A. 84: Werner Forman Archive, London/courtesy Entwistle Gallery, London. 85: Rod McIntosh, Houston. 86: Map by Dale Glasgow. 88: Hutchison Library, London. 90: Coll. Musée de l'Homme, Paris. 94: Bibliothèque Nationale, Paris. 99, 100: Hutchison Library, London. 101: © Dirk Bakker. 103: Werner Forman Archive, London/British Museum, London. 105: Superstock. 106: Werner Forman Archive, London/British Museum, London; André Held, Ecublens, Switzerland. 107: Lee Boltin—© British Museum, London. 109: Rod McIntosh, Houston. 111: André Held, Ecublens, Switzerland. 112, 113: André Held, Ecublens, Switzerland; © Dirk Bakker (2). 114: © Dirk Bakker. 115: André Held, Ecublens, Switzerland. 116: © British Museum, London; The Metropolitan Museum of Art, Gift of Mr. and Mrs. Klaus G. Perls, 1991 (1991.17.2). 117: The Metropolitan Museum of Art, The Michael C. Rockefeller Memorial Collection, Gift of Nelson A. Rockefeller, 1972 (1978.412.323). Photograph by Schecter Lee. 118: Timothy Beddow/The Hutchison Library, London. 120: Courtesy The Transvall Museum, photo: University of Pretoria. 122: Map by Dale Glasgow. 125: Art by Fred Holtz adapted from an illustration (modified) by Hank Iken from *The Swahili Corridor,* by Mark Horton, September 1987, copyright © 1987 by Scientific American, Inc. All Rights Reserved. 126: Werner Forman Archive, London—Werner Forman Archive, London/Tanzania National Museum, Dar es Salaam. 127: Shen Tu (1357-1434), Tribute Giraffe with Attendant, 1403-1424,

Philadelphia Museum of Art: Given by John T. Dorrance. 129: Dr. Mark Horton, Shropshire, England. 130, 131: Ashmolean Museum, Oxford, courtesy Department of Archives and Antiquities, Office of the President of Zanzibar, P.O. Box 116, Zanzibar. 132, 133: © Marc & Evelyne Bernheim/Woodfin Camp & Associates, New York. 135: Reprinted by permission from Peter S. Garlake, *The Early Islamic Architecture of the East African Coast,* Memoir 1 of the British Institute in Eastern Africa, Nairobi, 1966, and *The Kingdoms of Africa:* Equinox (Oxford) Ltd., 1990. 137: Superstock. 141: Gerald Cubitt, Cape Town, South Africa. 142: Robert Harding Picture Library, London—J. Rushmer/ZEFA Picture Library, London; Superstock. 143: © Jason Lauré/Woodfin Camp & Associates, New York. 144, 147: © Robert Holmes. 148: Courtesy The Oriental Institute of The University of Chica-

go—Leni Riefenstahl. 149: Photo Igor Delmas-Shango Productions, from *Art of Africa,* by J. Kerchache (Abrams); Georg Gerster/© 1994 Comstock, Inc. 150: Staatliche Museen zu Berlin-Preussischer Kulturbesitz, Museum für Völkerkunde; © Rijksmuseum voor Volkenkunde Leiden/photo: G. Jansen. 151: Rod McIntosh, Houston; Marcel Isy-Schwart/The Image Bank—The University Museum, University of Pennsylvania; photo: Angela Fisher/Robert Estall Photographs, Suffolk, England. 152: James L. Stanfield, © National Geographic Society—Anthony Ponter. 153: © M.& A. Kirtley/A.N.A.; photo Helen Haskell, courtesy Rod McIntosh. 154: Hutchison Library, London. 155: Georg Gerster/© 1994 Comstock, Inc. 156, 157: © Labelle Prussin; from Bourgeois and Pelos: *Spectacular Vernacular,* chapter 11, *Histories of the Great Mosques of Djenné.* 158, 159: Art by Paul Breeden.

BIBLIOGRAPHY

BOOKS

Adams, William Y. *Nubia: Corridor to Africa.* London: Allen Lane, 1977.

Anquandah, James. *Rediscovering Ghana's Past.* Essex, England: Longman, 1982.

Axelson, Eric. *Portuguese in South-East Africa, 1488-1600.* Johannesburg: C. Struik, 1973.

Bassani, Ezio, and William B. Fagg. *Africa and the Renaissance: Art in Ivory.* Edited by Susan Vogel. New York: Center for African Art, 1988.

Beach, D. N. *The Shona & Zimbabwe, 900-1850.* New York: Africana Publishing, 1980.

Ben-Amos, Paula. *The Art of Benin.* London: Thames and Hudson, 1980.

Bonnet, Charles. *Kerma, Royaume de Nubie.* Geneva: University of Geneva, 1990.

Breasted, Charles:
Ancient Records of Egypt: Historical Documents. Chicago: University of Chicago Press, 1906.

Pioneer to the Past: The Story of James Henry Breasted, Archaeologist. New York: Scribner's, 1943.

Burke, E. E. (ed.). *The Journals of Carl Mauch: His Travels in the Transvaal and Rhodesia, 1869-1872.* Translated by F. O. Bernhard. Salisbury: National Archives of Rhodesia, 1969.

Cable, Mary, and the Editors of Tree Communications. *The African Kings* (Treasures of the World series). New York: Stonehenge Press, 1983.

Carré, Jean-Noire. *Voyageurs et Écrivains Français en Égypte* (Vol. 1). Cairo: Institut Français d'Archéologie Orientale, 1956.

Chittick, Neville:
Kilwa: An Islamic Trading City on the East African Coast (Vols. 1 and 2). Nairobi, Kenya: British Institute in Eastern Africa, 1974.

Manda: Excavations at an Island Port on the Kenya Coast. Nairobi, Kenya: British Institute in Eastern Africa, 1984.

Connah, Graham:

African Civilizations. Cambridge: Cambridge University Press, 1987.

The Archaeology of Benin. Oxford: Clarendon Press, 1975.

Davidson, Basil:
African Civilization Revisited: From Antiquity to Modern Times. Trenton: Africa World Press, 1991.

The Lost Cities of Africa. Boston: Little, Brown, 1987.

Davidson, Basil, and the Editors of Time-Life Books. *African Kingdoms* (Great Ages of Man series). New York: Time Incorporated, 1966.

Davies, W. V. (ed.). *Egypt and Africa: Nubia from Prehistory to Islam.* London: British Museum Press, 1993.

DeMott, Barbara L. *Dogon Masks: A Structural Study of Form and Meaning.* Ann Arbor, Mich.: UMI Research Press, 1982.

Dunham, Dows. *The Royal Cemeteries of Kush:*
El Kurru (Vol. 1). Cambridge, Mass.: Harvard University Press, 1950.

Nuri (Vol. 2). Boston: Museum of Fine Arts, 1955.

Dunn, Ross E. *The Adventures of Ibn Battuta*. Berkeley: University of California Press, 1986.

Elliott, Kit. *Benin: An African Kingdom and Culture*. Minneapolis: Lerner Publications, 1979.

Emery, Walter B.:
Egypt in Nubia. London: Hutchinson of London, 1965.
Nubian Treasure. London: Methuen, 1948.

Eyo, Ekpo, and Frank Willett. *Treasures of Ancient Nigeria*. London: Royal Academy of Arts, 1980.

Ezra, Kate. *Royal Art of Benin*. New York: Harry N. Abrams, 1992.

Fagg, William. *Yoruba: Sculpture of West Africa*. New York: Alfred A. Knopf, 1982.

Fahim, Hussein M. *Egyptian Nubians: Resettlement and Years of Coping*. Salt Lake City: University of Utah Press, 1983.

Fisher, Angela. *Africa Adorned*. New York: Harry N. Abrams, 1984.

Fouché, Leo. *Mapungubwe: Ancient Bantu Civilization on the Limpopo*. Cambridge: Cambridge University Press, 1937.

Freeman-Grenville, G. S. P.:
The East African Coast. London: Rex Collings, 1975.
The Swahili Coast, 2nd to 19th Centuries. London: Variorum Reprints, 1988.

Freyer, Bryna. *Royal Benin Art*. Washington, D.C.: Smithsonian Institution Press, 1987.

Garlake, Peter S.:
The Early Islamic Architecture of the East African Coast. Nairobi, Kenya: Oxford University Press, 1966.
Early Zimbabwe: From the Matopos to Inyanga. Zimbabwe: Mambo Press, 1983.
Great Zimbabwe. London: Thames and Hudson, 1973.
The Kingdoms of Africa. New York: Peter Bedrick Books, 1978.
Life at Great Zimbabwe. Zimbabwe: Mambo Press, 1983.

Gillon, Werner. *A Short History of African Art*. London: Penguin Books, 1984.

Guiterman, Helen, and Briony Llewellyn. *David Roberts*. Oxford, England: Phaidon Press and Barbi-

can Art Gallery, 1986.

Hall, Martin. *Farmers, Kings, and Traders: The People of Southern Africa, 200-1860*. Chicago: University of Chicago Press, 1990.

Haynes, Joyce L. *Nubia: Ancient Kingdoms of Africa*. Boston: Museum of Fine Arts, 1992.

Herbert, Eugenia W. *Red Gold of Africa: Copper in Precolonial History and Culture*. Madison: University of Wisconsin Press, 1984.

Hintze, Fritz (ed.). *Meroitica: Africa in Antiquity, the Arts of Ancient Nubia and the Sudan*. Berlin: Akademie-Verlag, 1979.

Hochfield, Sylvia, and Elizabeth Riefstahl (eds.). *Africa in Antiquity* (2 vols.). Translated by Diana S. Peters and Charles M. Stern. Brooklyn: Brooklyn Museum, 1978.

Hodgkin, Thomas. *Nigerian Perspectives: An Historical Anthology*. London: Oxford University Press, 1975.

Huet, Michel. *The Dance, Art and Ritual of Africa*. New York: Random House, 1978.

Huffman, T. N.:
A Guide to the Great Zimbabwe Ruins. Salisbury: Trustees of the National Museums & Monuments of Rhodesia, 1976.
Symbols in Stone: Unravelling the Mystery of Great Zimbabwe. Johannesburg: Witwatersrand University Press, 1987.

Hugon, Anne. *The Exploration of Africa: From Cairo to the Cape*. Translated by Alexandra Cambell. New York: Harry N. Abrams, 1993.

James, T. G. H. (ed.). *Excavating in Egypt*. Chicago: University of Chicago Press, 1982.

Josephy, Alvin M. , Jr. (ed.). *The Horizon History of Africa*. New York: American Heritage, 1971.

July, Robert W. *Precolonial Africa: An Economic and Social History*. New York: Scribner's, 1975.

Keating, Rex:
Nubian Rescue. New York: Hawthorn, 1975.
Nubian Twilight. London: Rupert Hart-Davis, 1962.

Kendall, Timothy. *Kush: Lost Kingdom of the Nile*. Brockton, Mass.: Brockton Art Museum, 1982.

Kirkman, James:
Gedi. 8th edition. Mombasa, Kenya:

Rodwell Press, 1975.
Men and Monuments on the East African Coast. London: Lutterworth Press, 1964.

Levtzion, Nehemia. *Ancient Ghana and Mali*. New York: Africana Publishing, 1973.

MacQuitty, William. *Island of Isis: Philae, Temple of the Nile*. New York: Scribner's, 1976.

Mallows, Wilfrid. *The Mystery of the Great Zimbabwe: A New Solution*. New York: W. W. Norton, 1984.

Middleton, John. *The World of the Swahili: An African Mercantile Civilization*. New Haven: Yale University Press, 1992.

Mintz, Anita. *The Art of West African Kingdoms*. Edited by Dean Trackman. Washington, D.C.: Smithsonian Institution, 1987.

Moorehead, Alan. *The Blue Nile*. New York: Harper & Row, 1972.

Murray, Jocelyn (ed.). *Cultural Atlas of Africa*. New York: Facts On File, 1981.

The New Encyclopaedia Britannica (Vols. 2 and 6). Chicago: Encyclopaedia Britannica, 1974.

Oliver, Roland, and Brian M. Fagan. *Africa in the Iron Age*. Cambridge: Cambridge University Press, 1975.

Olson, Stacie, and Josef Wegner. *Ancient Nubia: Egypt's Rival in Africa*. Philadelphia: The University Museum, 1992.

The Oriental Institute. *The 1905-1907 Breasted Expeditions to Egypt and the Sudan: A Photographic Study* (Vol. 2). Chicago: University of Chicago Press, 1975.

Phillipson, David W. *African Archaeology*. Cambridge: Cambridge University Press, 1985.

Ponter, Anthony, and Laura Ponter. *Spirits in Stone: The New Face of African Art*. Sebastopol, Calif.: Ukama Press, 1992.

Reisner, George A. *Excavations at Kerma, Parts 1-3. Volume 5: Harvard African Studies*. Millwood, N.Y.: Kraus Reprint Co., 1975 (reprint of 1923 edition).

Renfrew, Colin, and Paul Bahn. *Archaeology*. New York: Thames and Hudson, 1991.

Riefenstahl, Leni. *The Last of the Nuba*. New York: Harper & Row, 1973.

Ryder, A. F. C. *Benin and the Euro-*

peans, 1485-1897. New York: Humanities Press, 1969.

Säve-Söderbergh, Torgny (ed.). *Temples and Tombs of Ancient Nubia.* New York: Thames and Hudson, 1987.

Schaedler, Karl-Ferdinand. *Weaving in Africa: South of the Sahara.* Translated by Leonid Prince Lieven and Judy Howell. Munich: Panterra Verlag, 1987.

Shaw, Thurstan:
Nigeria: Its Archaeology and Early History. London: Thames and Hudson, 1978.
Unearthing Igbo-Ukwu. Ibadan, Nigeria: Oxford University Press, 1977.

Shinnie, P. L. *Meroe: A Civilization of the Sudan.* New York: Frederick A. Praeger, 1967.

Snow, Philip. *The Star Raft: China's Encounter with Africa.* Ithaca, New York: Cornell University Press, 1988.

Sommerlatte, Herbert W. A. *Gold und Ruinen in Zimbabwe.* Gütersloh, Germany: Bertelsmann Fachzeitschriften, 1987.

Summers, Roger. *Ancient Mining in Rhodesia: And Adjacent Areas.* Salisbury, Rhodesia: Trustees of the National Museums of Rhodesia, 1969.

Sutton, John E. G. *A Thousand Years of East Africa.* Nairobi, Kenya: British Institute in Eastern Africa, 1990.

Taylor, John H. *Egypt and Nubia.* Cambridge, Mass.: Harvard University Press, 1991.

Trigger, Bruce G. *Nubia under the Pharaohs.* London: Thames and Hudson, 1976.

Voigt, Elizabeth A. *Mapungubwe: An Archaeozoological Interpretation of an Iron Age Community.* Pretoria, South Africa: Transvaal Museum, 1983.

Willett, Frank. *African Art: An Introduction.* London: Thames and Hudson, 1971.

Wilson, John A. *Signs and Wonders upon Pharaoh: A History of American Egyptology.* Chicago: University of Chicago Press, 1964.

PERIODICALS

Abercrombie, Thomas J. "Ibn Battuta: Prince of Travelers." *National Geographic,* December 1991.

Bonnet, Charles. "Excavations at Nubian Kerma, 1975-91." *Antiquity,* September 1992.

Cole, Herbert M. "Artistic and Communicative Values of Beads in Kenya and Ghana." *Bead Journal,* winter 1975.

Craddock, Paul. "Behind the Scenes." *British Museum Magazine,* summer 1991.

Drewal, Henry John, John Pemberton III, and Rowland Abiodun. "Yoruba: Nine Centuries of African Art and Thought." *African Arts,* November 1989.

Eluyemi, Omotoso. "Excavations at Isoya near Ile-Ife (Nigeria), in 1972." *West African Journal of Archaeology,* 1977.

Farrell, William E. "Nubians Yearn for Lost Lands on Nile and Some Have Managed to Go Back." *New York Times,* December 31, 1978.

Forbes, Dennis C. "A Great Find Revisited: The Tomb of Fanbearer Mahirpre." *KMT: A Modern Journal of Ancient Egypt,* fall 1993.

Horton, Mark:
"Early Muslim Trading Settlements on the East African Coast: New Evidence from Shanga." *Antiquaries Journal,* Vol. 66, 1988.
"The Swahili Corridor." *Scientific American,* September 1987.

Huffman, T. N. "The Rise and Fall of Zimbabwe." *Journal of African History,* 1972.

Kaplan, Flora Edouwaye S. "Images of the Queen Mother in Benin Court Art." *African Arts,* July 1993.

Kendall, Timothy:
"Jebel Barkal: Sacred Mountain of Kush." *Museum of Fine Arts, Boston,* 1993.
"Kingdom of Kush." *National Geographic,* November 1990.

Kirwan, I. P. "Rhapta, Metropolis of Azania." *Azania,* Vol. 21, 1986.

KMT: A Modern Journal of Ancient Egypt, fall 1992.

McIntosh, Roderick J., and Susan Keech McIntosh:
"Forgotten Tells of Mali." *Archaeology,* winter 1983.
"The Inland Niger Delta before the Empire of Mali: Evidence from Jenne-Jeno." *Journal of African History,* Vol. 22, 1981.
"Terracotta Statuettes from Mali." *African Arts,* February 1979.

McIntosh, Susan, and Roderick J. McIntosh:
"Finding West Africa's Oldest City." *National Geographic,* September 1982.
"From Stone to Metal: New Perspectives on the Later Prehistory of West Africa." *Journal of World Prehistory,* Vol. 2, no. 1, 1988.
"Recent Archaeological Research and Dates from West Africa." *Journal of African History,* Vol. 27, pp. 413-442, 1986.
"West African Prehistory." *American Scientist,* Vol. 69, no. 6, November-December 1981.

Posnansky, Merrick. "Dating Ghana's Earliest Art." *African Arts,* November 1979.

Roberts, David. "Nubia: The Unfolding Story of a Storied Land." *Smithsonian,* June 1993.

Shaw, Thurstan. "Those Igbo-Ukwu Radiocarbon Dates: Facts, Fictions and Probabilities." *Journal of African History,* Vol. 16, no. 4, 1975.

Sinclair, Paul J. J. "Archaeology in Eastern Africa: An Overview of Current Chronological Issues." *Journal of African History,* Vol. 32, pp. 179-219, 1991.

Willett, Frank. "Riches from Nigeria's Past." *Portfolio,* summer 1980.

OTHER SOURCES

Anquandah, James. "Ethnoarchaeological Clues to Ghana's Great Past and—a Greater Future?" Lecture. University of Ghana, Monographs and Papers in African Archaeology, no. 2, 1985.

Breasted, James H. "Journal of the University of Chicago Egyptian Expedition, 1906-1907." Unpublished journals. Books 1, 2, 3, 4, and 6.

"Frédéric Cailliaud." *Dictionnaire Illustré des Explorateurs Français du XX Siècle—Africa.* Entry on NUMA BROC, Éditions C.T.H.S., 1988.

Horton, Mark:
"The Archaeology of Islam in Eastern Africa." Lecture. Royal African Society, May 5, 1993.
"Facing Mecca at Shanga: Some

Problems in the Origins of Islam in Eastern Africa." Seminar. University of London, May 3, 1989.

Jolaoso, Olujimi. "Treasures of Ancient Nigeria: Legacy of 2000 Years." Exhibition opening address. Detroit Institute of Arts, January 14, 1980.

Kendall, Timothy:
"The Gebel Barkal Temples, 1989-90." Progress report on the work of the Museum of Fine Arts, Boston, Sudan Mission. Seventh International Conference for Nubian Studies, September 3-September 8, 1990.

"The Lure of the Nile: The American Discovery of Ancient Egypt." Essay. Museum of Fine Arts, Boston, n.d.

"Man and Metal in Ancient Nigeria." Exhibition publication. British Museum, September 1991.

Priese, Karl-Heinz. *The Gold of Meroe.* Catalog. The Metropolitan Museum of Art, New York, 1993.

Reisner, George Andrew. "Excavating the Tomb of King Taharka." Bulletin of the Museum of Fine Arts of 1918. Reprinted in "Explorations in Ancient Nubia," Boston Museum of Fine Arts.

Saleh, Mohamed, and Hourig Sourouzian. *The Egyptian Museum Cairo.* Catalog. Mainz, Germany: Verlag Philipp, 1987.

Shaw, Thurstan. "Bones in Africa: Presidential Address 1989." Proceedings of the Prehistoric Society 56, 1990.

INDEX